Teacher Induction That Works

Getting new teachers off to the right start is essential for teacher retention and student success. This book shows the nuts and bolts of induction that really works.

Drawing on the successful, research-based S.H.I.N.E. program, the authors demonstrate the key components for setting up or tweaking your new teacher induction program, including involving different staff members; remembering that induction is not an event but an ongoing process; considering the different phases of induction and the support and modeling needed along the way; finding appropriate mentors; helping new teachers juggle priorities; and more. As beginning teachers often leave due to classroom management struggles, this book also helps you give teachers the basics immediately so they're set up for success. In addition, the appendix offers a wealth of tools and templates to help you cover all the bases during your induction journey.

Whether you're an induction coordinator, mentor, professional development leader, principal, or superintendent, this practical resource will help you ensure your new teachers thrive so they can enjoy their roles and effectively reach students. When a program to support new teachers is made stronger, the accelerated growth and acclimation of new teachers can accelerate the growth of students too!

Tara Link is the developer and coordinator of the new teacher induction program S.H.I.N.E. (Supporting, Helping, & Inspiring New Educators) for the Moberly School District in Missouri. As a career K–12 educator and practitioner, she has served in many roles from a classroom teacher to learning leader and instructional coach. Her district was chosen as one of only two districts in the United States and among 15 in the entire world to be an example of visible learning implementation for Dr. John Hattie's work. Moberly School District has also been continuously highlighted by Dr. Harry Wong as an example in the education world of a research-based practice that when done well, creates results for student engagement and learning.

Beth Whitaker is a professor in the Department of Educational Leadership and Policy Analysis at the University of Missouri, Columbia. She is a former classroom teacher and principal in Missouri. During her tenure at Mizzou, Beth received the University of Missouri William T. Kemper Fellowship for Teaching Excellence, the College of Education and Human Development Golden Apple for Teaching Excellence, and the Outstanding College of Teaching Award. Beth was also an award-winning professor at Indiana State University prior to her employment at Mizzou.

Also Available from Routledge Eye On Education

www.routledge.com/k-12

Motivating & Inspiring Teachers: The Educational Leader's Guide for Building Staff Morale
Todd Whitaker, Beth Whitaker, and Dale Lumpa

Your First Year, 2nd Edition: How to Survive and Thrive as a New Teacher
Todd Whitaker, Katherine Whitaker, Madeline Whitaker Good

Classroom Management from the Ground Up
Todd Whitaker, Katherine Whitaker, Madeline Whitaker Good

Invest in Your Best: 9 Strategies to Grow, Support, and Celebrate Your Most Valuable Teachers
Todd Whitaker, Connie Hamilton, Joseph Jones, T.J. Vari

What Great Principals Do Differently, 3rd Edition: Twenty Things That Matter Most
Todd Whitaker

What Great Teachers Do Differently, 3rd Edition: Nineteen Things That Matter Most
Todd Whitaker

Dealing with Difficult Parents, 2nd Edition
Todd Whitaker and Douglas Fiore

Teacher Induction That Works

A Lasting Impact From Day One

Tara Link and Beth Whitaker

Routledge
Taylor & Francis Group

NEW YORK AND LONDON

Designed cover image: Getty images

First published 2025
by Routledge
605 Third Avenue, New York, NY 10158

and by Routledge
4 Park Square, Milton Park, Abingdon, Oxon, OX14 4RN

Routledge is an imprint of the Taylor & Francis Group, an informa business

© 2025 Tara Link and Beth Whitaker

The right of Tara Link and Beth Whitaker to be identified as authors of this work has been asserted in accordance with sections 77 and 78 of the Copyright, Designs and Patents Act 1988.

All rights reserved. The purchase of this copyright material confers the right on the purchasing institution to photocopy or download pages which bear the support material icon and a copyright line at the bottom of the page. No other parts of this book may be reprinted or reproduced or utilised in any form or by any electronic, mechanical, or other means, now known or hereafter invented, including photocopying and recording, or in any information storage or retrieval system, without permission in writing from the publishers.

Trademark notice: Product or corporate names may be trademarks or registered trademarks, and are used only for identification and explanation without intent to infringe.

Library of Congress Cataloging-in-Publication Data
Names: Link, Tara, author. | Whitaker, Beth, 1960- author.
Title: Teacher induction that works : a lasting impact from day one / Tara Link and Beth Whitaker.
Description: New York, NY : Routledge, 2025. | Series: Routledge eye on education | Includes bibliographical references.
Identifiers: LCCN 2024040594 (print) | LCCN 2024040595 (ebook) | ISBN 9781032763514 (hardback) | ISBN 9781032730356 (paperback) | ISBN 9781003487470 (ebook)
Subjects: LCSH: First year teachers–United States. | Teacher effectiveness–United States. | Teachers–Professional relationships–United States.
Classification: LCC LB2844.1.N4 L56 2025 (print) | LCC LB2844.1.N4 (ebook) | DDC 371.14/12–dc23/eng/20241211
LC record available at https://lccn.loc.gov/2024040594
LC ebook record available at https://lccn.loc.gov/2024040595

ISBN: 978-1-032-76351-4 (hbk)
ISBN: 978-1-032-73035-6 (pbk)
ISBN: 978-1-003-48747-0 (ebk)

DOI: 10.4324/9781003487470

Typeset in Palatino
by Deanta Global Publishing Services, Chennai, India

Access the Support Material: Routledge.com/9781032763514

Support Material

The appendix items in this book are also available as free downloads on our website, so you can easily print them and use them in your own educational setting. To access the resources, go to www.routledge.com/9781032763514 and click on the link that says Support Material.

Contents

Acknowledgements xi
Meet the Authors xiii

Introduction 1

SECTION 1: LET'S GET THIS JOURNEY STARTED
Let's Meet the Newbies 9
1 The Launch 11
2 Gold Star Moments 17
3 It Takes a Village 21

SECTION 2: MAKING IT HAPPEN
4 We Have the Who, Now to the How 29
5 All Onboard! Onboarding and Saying Hello 33
6 Modeling Is Orientation 40
7 The Hub of Induction 52
8 Learning by Observing 61
9 Peripherals Are Essential 70

SECTION 3: POLISHING THE APPLE
10 Celebrating and Reflecting 85
11 Support the Supporters 88
12 Love a Teaching Life 96
13 Additional Considerations 101

SECTION 4: IN AND OUT OF THE CLASSROOM

14 The Little Things Are the Big Things 107
15 It's Not About Being the Best, Just Being Better 114
16 Elevate What You Want to Grow 123
    Conclusion: Stoplights. 126

Appendix. 129
References 153

Acknowledgements

From Tara Link:

To the two who first believed in this book, thank you! Alaina Link, here you go. I give you full credit for planting the seed many years ago and in your persistent way, continuing to remind me. Beth Whitaker, your guiding light, encouragement, gentle nudge, and partner in this journey is a treasured gift.

How lucky I was to meet you in the hallway many years ago! Moberly School District will forever be home and I will forever be a Spartan. The leadership through the years, fellow instructional coaches, my colleagues, community, and all of the beginning teachers for whom I had a front row seat to their growth as a professional, thank you. Words to describe the support throughout my career are hard to come by for a district that has truly helped to make this a reality. Each of you has had an impact on this book and my growth and learning as a professional. And last, but not least, my family and biggest supporters. Troy, Anna Kate, and Alaina, you are my greatest joy, blessing, encouragement, and world. My mom, Kay, your love and support since day one for me and my family got me started. To my dad, Dave Harris, I know you are smiling from above. My start in education and ability to write this book started with your influence. TGgg.

From Beth Whitaker:

First and foremost, I must acknowledge the expertise and brilliance of my co-author. Tara Link represents the very best in education, and I am deeply honored to have been able to work with her on this project. Her knowledge of new teacher induction and onboarding is second to none. Her dedicated work focused on teacher success is rich and practical. Her ideas and guidance in this book will benefit everyone involved in teacher induction.

I am blessed to exist within a family of educators. My husband, Todd, is a constant source of support, guidance, and inspiration. I am extremely blessed to have him as my partner in life. Our children, Katherine, Madeline, and Harrison, have each found their way into teaching and we couldn't be prouder. They are all expanding their work in education related fields but remain steadfast in their belief that effective teaching is foundational to student success. All four of these individuals inspire my work and life every single day.

In closing, I must acknowledge the hard and necessary work that all teachers engage in daily. They are truly rockstars and our world is a better place because they choose to teach.

Meet the Authors

Tara Link has spent her education career finding ways to help students and teachers alike discover the joy in learning and teaching. She strives to help educators find ways to bridge research and classroom practical application of strategies to support student learning. She is the creator and coordinator of the Moberly School District S.H.I.N.E. (Supporting, Helping, & Inspiring New Educators) which has received recognition and publication  in books and articles from Dr. John Hattie and Dr. Harry Wong. Her work has been shared through new teacher professional development workshops and national, state, and local conferences. Tara has supported her Missouri school district in various roles, including innovation instructional coach, education technology coach, federal programs support, curriculum work, and professional development chair. Her experience also includes teaching at the high school, middle school, and elementary level as a classroom teacher and reading interventionist.

Tara is married to Troy and they are the proud parents of two amazing daughters: Anna Kate and Alaina.

Dr. Beth Whitaker is a teaching professor in the Department of Educational Leadership and Policy Analysis at the University of Missouri, Columbia. Dr. Whitaker earned her undergraduate degree from Central Methodist University, her M.Ed. and Ed.S. degrees from the University of Missouri, Columbia, and her Ph.D. from Indiana State University.

Beth is a former classroom teacher and principal in Missouri. During her tenure as an administrator, her school was awarded the Missouri Gold Star and National Blue Ribbon for excellence in education. Dr. Whitaker has been published in the areas of school climate, principal leadership, and staff motivation and morale. She teaches K–12 leadership courses and supervises administrator interns at Mizzou. During her tenure at Mizzou, Beth has received the following teaching awards: College of Education and Human Development *Golden Apple for Teaching Excellence,* College of Education and Human Development *Outstanding College of Teaching Award* and the University of Missouri *William T. Kemper Fellowship for Teaching Excellence.*

Prior to returning to Missouri seven years ago, Dr. Whitaker was a professor in the Bayh College of Education and founding director of The Faculty Center for Teaching Excellence at Indiana State University in Terre Haute, Indiana. While at ISU, Beth received the *Caleb Mills Distinguished Teaching Award, Holmstedt Distinguished Professorship, Kinser Faculty Award,* and the *President's Award from the Indiana State Principal's Association.*

Her husband, Todd, is her constant source of inspiration, and they have collaborated on numerous books and presentations. Most importantly, they are the very proud parents of Katherine, Madeline, and Harrison.

Introduction

Why This Book?

From Tara ...
Learning has always been my passion. Bringing the joy of learning to students and the window into the world of possibilities and hope that can accompany the ride, led to thirteen years in classrooms as a teacher. A new spark was ignited when I was presented with the opportunity to support beginning teachers in my school district. Similar to numerous other school districts, the need to attract and retain teachers led to the idea of trying something not as common at the time—creating a new teacher induction program. Taking a chance, a small semi-rural district in Moberly, Missouri, decided to dedicate me, a classroom teacher, to the role of supporting new hires and, most especially, first- and second-year teachers. A conference handout from a presentation of a much larger district was the genesis to prompt the idea. It would be a one-year trial program. Inspiration from the research of larger districts already on this path and a vision to support our newest professionals set the stage to a lasting program. With the school board's approval and a strong commitment to the development of beginning teachers, the induction program was established and evolved, accompanied by valuable lessons along the way. Through the tireless work, support, and contributions of many great Moberly Public School district, building, and teacher leaders, including a great team of instructional coaches, the Moberly School District S.H.I.N.E. (Supporting, Helping, & Inspiring New Teachers) program began.

Seventeen plus years later, the program has continued to grow and develop along with the evolving needs of the new beginning teachers. It has sustained its function because many great leaders of education in the Moberly School District became a part of the program in providing support and valuing the purpose. Being the person "on the ground," working directly with new teachers, and developing the program, I have had a unique opportunity to gain a comprehensive perspective of the joys and challenges that arise from the many facets of working with new and beginning teachers. From this vantage point, it became evident that celebrations and obstacles go hand in hand, each offering valuable insights shared in this book. In addition, along the way, learning from other school districts and people also supporting new teachers has provided a broad perspective of ideas.

From Beth ...

My journey in education as a teacher, principal, and a professor teaching future teachers and principals has taught me the importance of recognizing that new members of a group, class, school, or district need a strong scaffold into the new organization. Leaders often have keen awareness that each new hire enters with prior knowledge and expertise. These leaders must also be aware that these new hires don't have institutional knowledge, an understanding of cultural norms/values, and a roadmap to success in their new home. These needs must be met by people that have employed them, guided by intentional planning and implementation of induction and onboarding programs. These programs are often not at the top of "to do" lists for organizational leaders. Recruitment and retention of effective employees must always be a high priority for schools, districts, and organizations. Many leaders spend a great deal of time on recruiting these individuals, but minimal time is spent creating systems to retain them. One of the most powerful tools for retention is making sure that a meaningful, ongoing, and robust induction process is created and put in place.

    I had the pleasure of hearing Tara Link speak to a graduate school class several years ago. She shared her induction process and programming with a room full of highly engaged graduate students. Honestly, the person probably the most in awe and engaged was the professor guiding the class … me. I remember telling her at the time that her approach to this important work needed to be shared. She had been presenting at regional, state, and national meetings to audiences that had many questions and wanted follow-up with her. For the past eight years, I have invited her to speak to my class, and each year I told her the same thing: *This work needs to be shared with a larger audience!* After a long lunch together a couple of years ago, we began to imagine this book and my job as head "encourager" was launched. Tara's rich insights on induction from design to delivery will be a gift to every person reading this book.

It has been an honor to collaborate with an extremely talented and dedicated educator on such an important topic. I guarantee there is something for everyone in this book. From small tweaks to what you currently have in place, to complete induction program design, readers will find something that will strengthen the important task of creating a process to support and guide new members of your organization. If setting up your newly hired staff for success is important to you, this book will supply you with the ideas and tools to help them thrive in their new organizational home.

Who Is This Book For?

1. Districts of all sizes!

Superintendents, District Leaders: District leaders can use this resource to guide the district and buildings in supporting the vision, purpose, resources, and people to support new hires. When forming a team or the right people to work for the district to assess goals, needs, and implementation of supporting new hires, leaders can use this book as a tool for supporting the thinking, asking of questions, and considerations to best advocate and implement the work.

2. Schools of all sizes!

Building Principals: This book helps principals determine what messages and components are critical for a particular school in supporting your community of professionals joining the building. It's important to identify what resources are needed, who are the people to help make it a reality, what culture we want to build or sustain, and what are the steps for doing so. You'll be given support to answer questions such as: How do we create a village of support/team focused on success for teachers *and* students? What tools and ideas can make it happen and what leadership roles are *needed to do so?*

3. Formal and informal leaders!

<u>Instructional Coaches, Mentors, Grade Level, Department/ Professional Development Chairs, Committee Members</u>: You'll learn about ideas, tools, and considerations for supporting new teachers, understand the critical importance of their roles, and how to help them improve upon or implement ideas.

The purpose of new teacher induction is to create a systematic and intentional process that supports new educators from the moment they sign their contract with the district until they complete their first school year of teaching and beyond. Induction for new teachers can include formal and informal processes that address various aspects of the profession. For beginning teachers, it is a crucial period during which the most novice teachers must learn much of the art of and some of the science of teaching—while actually teaching.

A brand-new teacher must be adequately prepared for having their own classroom and students, and making hundreds of decisions a day. Everyone was once a student. Yet, switching to the role of a teacher creates a whole new view of reality. No other profession with the task of educating has such a tall task to perform right out of the gates with only a 6-, 8-, or 12-week internship of quasi-experience. For some, the internship may be even less or not at all depending on the situation. So, what can we do, no matter what size the school or district or the amount of resources available to help make this happen? Change is an inevitable part of the teaching profession. Yet, amidst the changes in classrooms and students over the years, certain common elements have remained consistent. No matter the size, location, or any other factors that make the school or district unique, all beginning teachers can and should be supported at all levels. It might be a mentor, grade or subject level team members, principals, instructional coaches, and even the office staff fulfilling that role.

Schools have a vested interest in designing induction opportunities tailored to their mission and vision of success. Creating a sense of purpose, unity, and commitment among new teachers can help lead to improved teacher effectiveness, retention, and student outcomes. The traditional approach of a single new faculty meeting and basic support is no longer sufficient. The goal is not merely to secure a teacher's commitment for a second year but to support them in becoming successful, valued members of the school community so they can best support the students. We can help our newest teachers navigate the initial hurdles and minimize the potential roadblocks that may arise by providing the necessary resources and timely support. We can support a new teacher in our educational setting by knowing the important things to consider and developing a plan. This comprehensive approach not only aids in recruiting and retaining teachers but, most importantly, in supporting the success of students. When we can find ways to make the path a little smoother or the bumps fewer, the teachers can do their jobs better and students have more opportunities to be their best.

With so many components to educating students in a classroom, a key question becomes: How do we communicate what is essential? We can tell our new teachers, or we can show them. Providing support, learning, and opportunities to practice and succeed are part of a well-planned process. How can we work to make the key ideas and most important goals of a district, school, or team more than just a transfer of information, but transformational for both teachers and students? A recipe when cooking is a guide to follow. It is the chef who brings the art of using spices and key actions that impact the end result. The ideas, thoughts, and suggestions in this book serve as the recipe. It will be the readers and their thinking that create the product for each place for which new teachers are beginning.

It is essential to realize the importance of connected support from all levels. At the organizational level, the district wants to provide an overview of expectations and practices to have continuity across all schools and settings. The building level is essential because that is where the majority of the needs of new staff members will arise. When there is a challenging student situation, the new teacher cannot wait until the district's next monthly new teacher meeting occurs to learn what to do. The pace in a classroom and school moves so quickly that there is a need for immediate support. And, depending on the size of the school, the instructional coach, department chair, grade level leader, mentor, or informal colleague may be the easiest and most available near-term contact. When these differing components work together cohesively, it greatly increases the likelihood of a new staff member's success.

Section 1
LET'S GET THIS JOURNEY STARTED

Let's Meet the Newbies

Meet Matt, an eager first-year teacher ready to launch his career as a 5th grade teacher. He excelled in college as a student, often engaging in dialogue with professors and fellow students about current and systemic educational issues. He read many books about the schools and teachers who had impacted students' lives in ways every teacher imagines themselves doing as their life calling. Matt spent many hours beyond student teaching, working with children in camps, after school programs, tutoring, and other youth events with a passion and enthusiasm to do more. He was ready for his first job.

Hannah had also excelled in college boasting a strong GPA and positive reviews from her cooperating teacher for student teaching in high school English. She could excitedly discuss writing and literature and ideas for sharing it with students. Her personality was one of kindness and eagerness to be a teacher sharing her passion to inspire students.

Marcos was a great paraprofessional in the building for several years. He worked in many classrooms in coordination with the teacher to assist students who have IEPs or need additional support. Due to a shortage of teachers, Marcos was recruited to become a long-term substitute teacher serving in the role of a full-time teacher while working to obtain teacher certification.

All three teachers have a genuine passion for education.

By October of their first year of teaching, these first-year teachers were second guessing their choice of profession. This was not the way any of them envisioned teaching would unfold or the experience they were anticipating. Working so hard to be prepared, feeling like their background experience was helpful, and having a passion for their chosen profession had misled them in ways they never anticipated. Sure, they knew it was going to be hard work planning lessons, creating materials for students, and providing redirection for students not meeting the expectations clearly lined out on the first few days of school. But having students disrupt class by talking incessantly when reminded repeatedly to stop? Papers to grade and meetings to attend when their planning period is anything other than planning time? Not to mention students who are falling behind due to a variety of reasons including absences, assignments not turned in, and failed assessments. The looming dates of grades being due along with parent teacher conferences on the horizon seemed to be the final pressures that kept coming up in the dizzying stir of conversations and reminders in meetings and emails. Exhaustion and fatigue seemed to be setting in as the weeks progressed. The initial excitement and anticipation they felt were overshadowed by the stress and frustration of the daily teaching grind.

Unfortunately, the experiences described above are not uncommon, as even the most talented and prepared new teachers often face similar difficulties. To anyone who has worked as an administrator, instructional coach, mentor, or with a beginning teacher, these situations can sound familiar. The seemingly most talented college graduates or non-traditional new teachers entering the profession seem to face similar challenges as a beginning teacher. Even teachers with experience joining a new school or district have additional stressors that impact the launching of their career in a new environment. The good news is that there are many things that can be done in any school or school district to provide support and help ease the challenges of entering one of the most critical professions.

Why teacher retention is challenging doesn't have a simple answer. Leading teacher attrition researcher Associate Professor Philip Riley from the Australian Catholic University in 2017 wrote, "It's an issue of complexity and of cost. We simply don't have the sophisticated systems in place to record all the nuances associated with teachers as they leave and shift within the profession" (Stroud, 2017).

This is not a book designed to attempt to answer that question or debate the challenges the education profession faces. It is a practical guide to ideas that have been implemented or researched to provide schools of all sizes with the tools and resources to best support their newest teachers.

1
The Launch

My journey to develop a long-standing new teacher induction program began with a conference handout and a year timeline. Next I conducted much research and adapted many ideas from new teacher programs in several large districts from around the United States. This was made possible by strong school district support to put ideas into practice and figure out what works best, mostly through trial and error and based on the needs of new teachers. Over time, through years of working closely with novice teachers across all grade levels, I have gained valuable insights into the key components of supporting new teachers, and especially beginning teachers. Many of these ideas and understandings are applicable to all new teachers, regardless of their experience level. This is particularly true of the first two parts of the induction process. Once the school year is underway, the primary focus is beginning teachers, although some parts are also fitting for all new teachers. As educational leaders collaborate to enhance their support for new hires, there are pivotal questions and components to consider, whether you are refining existing programs or embarking on the journey of establishing entirely new initiatives.

Inductees are often referred to as persons chosen for a hall of fame or honorable society based on high achievements. Each year, schools induct new teachers into their teams, buildings, and districts. When the people who choose such a noble and influential profession choose to come into your school and district, induct them with the esteem and preparation to guide their new path. Having a well-planned and executed new teacher induction plan in place can make a difference for the students, teachers, and administrators in a school or district of any size. Each school district has its own key components to be discovered to provide the best support. When a teacher joins a district and starts teaching in a school—either as a beginning teacher or as an experienced teacher new to the building—the structures in place to support them can make a big difference, not only during the start of the year, but throughout the entire year.

According to Simon Sinek (*Start with Why: How Great Leaders Inspire Action*, 2009), identifying the "why" is paramount to inspiring others. Every organization—and every person's career—operates on three levels: what we do, how we do it, and why we do it. A district or school must first have a grasp on the underlying reasons for supporting new teachers and be able to pinpoint what essential aspects need to be prioritized. Then it's important to identify methods for implementation and the key individuals involved in bringing these plans to fruition. Each of these will be discussed with ideas to follow.

> Having a well-planned and executed new teacher induction plan in place can make a difference for the students, teachers, and administrators in a school or district of any size.

Having a clear and well-articulated purpose or "why" for supporting new teachers can serve as a north star when navigating unchartered territory and can serve as a guide in decision making. If you are looking at a tall oak tree or a beautiful new house, what is above ground, visible, and appealing to the eye is built upon a robust root system or strong foundation. A successful new teacher induction program is much the same way. Clearly knowing why it's important to invest time, money, and additional resources will only strengthen the foundation from which new ideas are built or old ones continue. Having the key elements in place to build upon will ensure a long-lasting and effective program. Making sure that everyone who is a part of the work understands the "why" behind the work is also important.

Teacher recruitment and retention are often a significant priority for a school and district. This can sometimes be perceived as primarily an administrative concern. A vital support element can sometimes be overlooked as the teachers and staff are essential players in this equation as well. While recruiting teachers and providing them with the support to stay is critical, so is the understanding that stronger teachers lead to stronger students. Knowing that "Support for teachers is support for students" also forms the foundational purpose of a strong new teacher induction program.

Adopting a proactive and pragmatic approach to new teacher induction entails beginning with an assessment of the district and leaders' beliefs, mission, and current reality. An important first step is bringing together a team of educational leaders at the district, school building, or department/grade levels to build upon your new teacher induction plan and support. Having a variety of persons from different years of experience and roles can provide great insight. This group can help provide insight, ideas, feedback, and clarity to the goals, needs, and ideas for your induction process. As your planning team comes together, it's crucial to address these questions and genuinely grasp the "why" behind your efforts.

Taking Inventory of Where You Are

Ideas for getting started. As the planning team gathers, focus on the questions and stay on topic. It will be easy for the conversation to migrate to solutions, and there will be time for this later. This list of questions is a place to start. Choose a few to focus on that meet your particular induction goal(s) for this planning session. In your district, building, content area/grade level:

- ♦ What is the benefit of strong support to someone getting started in a career in your school and district? Who knows this?
- ♦ Why is recruiting and retaining quality teachers important?

- Why should a teacher, building administrator, central office administrators, technology coordinators, administrative assistants, and custodians know the district "why" of supporting the new hires?
- How do we currently quickly identify the strengths of our newest teachers?
- What are the indicators of a successful first or second year of teaching?
- What has been a common challenge for new teachers in the past?
- What patterns have you noticed with these challenges? (could be subject area, grade level, age group focused, time of year focused)
- What does it feel like to be new and overwhelmed? What are signs of this? What might be easily hidden?
- What is currently in place to support new teachers who are struggling versus high functioning new teachers?
- What makes our district/school/team unique?
- What are the most important things for a new hire to know and do to be successful on day 1, month 1, quarter 1, etc.?
- What are commonly known areas of struggles for new hires? Beginning teachers?
- What are the hidden rules of our district/school/team?
- Why should all employees want to support and assist a new hire?

It would be very tempting during this discussion to start coming up with ideas for solving any problems that might arise or debating the answers. There will be time for this later. Right now, focus on taking inventory on where you currently are. Take in all ideas; many perspectives will be important for consideration.

Now that you have an inventory, you can answer the last question, "Why should all employees want to support and assist a new hire?"

A Process, Not an Event

Establishing or reinforcing the existing structures and involving the key stakeholders in the development will be important now that you have a clearer understanding of why you will be investing time and energy in new teacher support. New teacher support is not a one- to five-day event at the start of school for the new hires; that is orientation. A variety of events throughout the induction process include contacting the new staff members upon hiring, orientation at the beginning of the school year, and professional development throughout the year. The intentional thinking to support the planning process, and events to follow are what will provide the impact and support for your "why." This is why induction is a process, not an event.

It is highly likely that most school districts will have some pieces already in place for supporting new teachers. Improving certain events or adding ideas to the process can enhance or contribute to your goal of quality new teacher support. As you seek new ideas or make changes, consider taking your approach to growth one step further by looking through a new lens or in a way never considered previously.

> New teacher support is not a one- to five-day event at the start of school for the new hires; that is orientation.

Sometimes being able to view what is already in place in a new way can help you discover something new. French novelist Marcel Proust wrote, "The real act of discovery consists not in finding new lands but in seeing with new eyes" (Shaker, 2015). This mindset has been called vuja de, the opposite of the unique feeling of déjà vu—when you feel like a moment that is happening has happened before, yet there is no evidence to support it. Vuja de is the idea of taking something common, familiar, or routine and looking at it with new eyes or as if it was happening for the first time (Berger, n.d.). For example, walk into your school building as if you had never been there before. What would you notice? Look at your website as if you had not seen it before or knew nothing about your school district or classroom.

This would be much like the perspective of a new hire in your district. Being willing to look at new teacher induction strategies through a different lens can be a catalyst for making changes and inviting a fresh perspective that might not have been otherwise recognized.

Equally, or possibly more important, is the quality of induction at the building level. If a district has a great induction program and the building doesn't, it could have limited value. If the building has a great induction program, whether the district does or not, is much less important. The building level is really an essential piece. Obviously coordinating them is a real win. That is where the most immediate feedback and support can be consistently provided. An additional valuable role of the district leadership is to help each school and principal have a personal and effective ongoing program in their building setting that works in tandem with the district's program.

Key Takeaways

- Take the time to get a clear picture of your current reality to help with planning.
- Gather a team with a variety of perspectives to take inventory of where you are.
- Strive for induction at all levels.
- Use vuja de to approach with new eyes the areas you would like to grow.

2
Gold Star Moments

Have you ever had an unexpected moment or event that shifted your perspective or elevated an experience? What does it take to help someone feel like a "gold star" member?

Our family vacation took us on a plane to a large city. The hecticness of traveling three hours to an airport, navigating the airport, flying for several hours, and then figuring out how to get our rental car took an exhausted toll on our family. We were the hungry, weary travelers off to an already "tired before we start" family vacation. Facing a long drive ahead, we found the rental car kiosk in the airport. Keep in mind, we did not fly or rent cars on a regular basis. The customer service representative dutifully looked up our reservation and replied to me with an upbeat voice, "Oh honey, no need to stop here. You are a gold star member! You go down the elevator and pick out any car you want!" Somewhat hesitantly, we dutifully followed her directions and landed in a parking garage full of cars. Again, not sure of ourselves, we found a person working in a small office and questioned what we should be doing. Again, we heard, "You are a gold star member. Pick out any car you want and have a great vacation!" Our travel weary family suddenly believed we truly were gold stars worthy of choosing any car as we excitedly exited the airport. Two employees that day made us feel like we were important customers. Our mindset shifted from the dread of a long drive to chuckles of being gold star members who got to

DOI: 10.4324/9781003487470-5

pick out their own car without waiting in a long line. The excitement of being a Gold Star member is what we want for our new hires. The goal is to have them join the school district as valued members of a community of professionals and *to* feel supported when navigating the ups and downs of their journey.

All educators have a first year in the profession, along with the memories and learning to go with it. Some may have stories they enjoy sharing or find humor in situations, while others may wish there were moments they could forget or would never want someone to know. It is no secret that the first year as an educator can feel like trying to fly a plane and build it at the same time while in a thunderstorm, and none of the passengers have their seat belts on. Suddenly, the beginning teacher is in charge of a group of students all on their own. No matter how great the student teaching experience (if there even was one), all their prior experiences did not prepare them for the unanticipated day-to-day challenges. Working hard to be the educator you have always hoped and dreamed to be while figuring things out on the fly makes the beginning years of being a teacher difficult. There's the constant influx of new information that can seem overwhelming, not to mention all the new faces of students and colleagues watching. No matter how great the teacher preparation program was at college or the experiences prior to getting your own classroom, the bridge between the two realities can be much less stable than anticipated. This is the common story of the beginning teacher.

> The goal is to have them join the school district as valued members of a community of professionals and to feel supported when navigating the ups and downs of their journey.

Relivables and Repeatables

Gold Star moments are the relivable moments a teacher will go back to days, months, and years later when talking about experiences in their career. Some may be planned moments created with intentionality, and others will be spontaneous events that will just happen in education. These are moments that will include students, colleagues, parents, or all of them together. It only takes a short time in education to start building upon those. We want to make the most of helping build the positive relivable moments as an education professional in your setting.

Relivables

Start by making a list of the relivables that are already a part of your school and district. Relivables are events and activities that occur on a regular basis and add positive momentum to district and school climate. These can be school traditions such as homecoming, yearly culture building events, or actions already in place such as a welcome phone call or note from the superintendent, principal, or team leader. Coordinating these things, even if multiple levels are involved, can provide a richer tapestry of welcome. By first considering what you already have in place, you may find you don't need to reinvent the wheel but can build upon what you are currently doing. Specific ideas have been intentionally left out early in this book to help you examine your own resources before you're influenced by the ideas presented. (See Thinking Guide #1 in the Appendix. In this guide, ideas are shared for each component of the induction process. You can use a copy of the Thinking Guide as a place to gather new ideas throughout the book.)

Repeatables

Repeatables are predictable and serve a different purpose. What are the things you repeat yearly to new hires and employees in general? What are common questions asked each year? What are the routines and procedures that are just that—routine? These are the repeatables. Use the Thinking Guide to help you find current repeatables for your district, school, or team.

Again, specific ideas or suggestions have been intentionally left out to help you examine your own resources first and not be limited by ideas presented. In other words, you may come up with creative new ideas that would not be considered if other ideas were initially suggested.

Repeatables need a place to live. It may be a website, digital folder, or even a paper copy in a binder. This is the resource provided to new hires (as well as to returning teachers) that can be referenced when a question arises. Regardless of how long a person has been in education, the beginning of the school year can feel like drinking through a fire hose—all the information comes rushing out at once. For new hires, this can be particularly overwhelming. The overload of information and trying to determine what is a priority to act upon or pay close attention to can lead to uncertainty. Trying to remember due dates, forms to turn in, and videos to watch can be a lot to juggle among the other parts of getting ready for a school year and preparing for the day-to-day work in the classroom. Resources can be available around the clock to refer back to during those moments when no one else is around.

Having relivables and repeatables identified at all levels—district, building, and so on—can help everyone understand the particular things that should be introduced and emphasized at each level. This way we can avoid unintentional repetition and identify gaps in new teacher support.

Key Takeaways

- The goal is to find ways both big and small to help your newest teachers feel like valued members of your learning community.
- Relivables at the district and building level are the moments you want teachers to remember fondly.
- Repeatables are the common pieces of information that teachers need to remember or may have questions about. These become available at any time through easy-to-access resources.

3

It Takes a Village

Teams that win seldom owe their success to a lone member. The significance of supportive players, coaches, and managers cannot be overstated, as they all contribute to a team's triumph. An orchestra relies on each musician and their instrument performing their part, guided by a conductor to create harmonious melodies. The collective focus is on a goal, with each orchestra member contributing uniquely to create beautiful music unobtainable alone. In much the same way, the adage "it takes a village" holds true when nurturing a novice teacher.

Within this village, several key players and contributors assume pivotal roles. The question arises: Who will drive the realization of your district's, school's, or team's purpose to make happen the "why" of new teacher induction? Perhaps there's a designated individual, like a principal, the superintendent, an instructional coach, a grade level leader, a mentor, or the teacher in the room next door or across the hallway overseeing the smooth initiation of new hires, or it could be the collaborative effort of a professional development committee. Everyone can have an important role in supporting new teachers. The significance lies in the collective commitment to supporting new teachers, much like the village raising a child.

The more defined the roles become for the support members, the stronger an induction program will be. Think about all the people each day who help a building to run smoothly. Some may

DOI: 10.4324/9781003487470-6

be there every day, others may come and go occasionally or as needed. The village of support, comprising various individuals who may be consistently present or occasional helpers, plays a vital role in shaping the program's success.

Identifying and assembling this village helps achieve the program's goals. But what exactly are the roles and core messages of each village member? Clearly define and communicate these roles to foster effective teamwork. It would be easy to skip over this part, perhaps thinking many of the roles are implied or obvious in your district. As time passes, people change positions, and the life of school happens, this foundational component can become murky when least expected, leading to a gap that could grow into a canyon without a clear plan in place.

> The village of support, comprising various individuals who may be consistently present or occasional helpers, plays a vital role in shaping the program's success.

With clear roles in place and in action, the practice of supporting new teachers seamlessly integrates into the daily operations and eventually forms or permeates the culture. The team becomes fortified, and supporting new hires evolves into an intrinsic value and practice. As newcomers and especially budding teachers experience this support, they eventually embrace the roles of village members for those who follow them. The mentoring program's capacity grows, and a culture of support takes root becoming an integral part of the routine—the embodiment of "it's just what we do around here."

Who are key players in your village and why are they important? What do they need to know about their role? As you begin to think about your "village of support" for new teachers, some key contributors for your planning may come to mind: superintendent, personnel/human resource coordinator, principals, mentor teachers, and team leaders/department chairs. Yet, there can be more critical support members that you overlooked: the building secretaries, custodians, technology support, food services, and community members who are also an important part of the village.

The custodian and administrative assistants/secretaries may be some of the first people to welcome a new hire and help them become settled into their room or space. They are the keepers of important information on how a building runs and how to access necessary materials. If we can ensure that the classroom computer and any interactive technology are ready to go with login information and working devices before a new hire arrives, it can be one less obstacle for them to launch a smooth start. Having codes already entered into the copy machine and other useful resources is time saved for a teacher. Articulating the importance of each of these roles and key information to share can help alleviate the possible anxiety of a new hire having to ask questions that may feel burdensome. The cafeteria is a part of a daily school routine that has to run like clockwork, yet can be a mystery if you do not know the system. Plus, we all want to eat food that others prepare! The food service workers can become part of the team to welcome the newest members and help them navigate an overwhelming energy hub of quickly moving food, kids, adults, voices, objects, and people.

Collectively, the resources of a village are numerous and vital. These are the people doing the work each day who can become leaders and supporters to help a new professional or employee become their best for students.

Ideas for Getting Started

- ♦ List all of the people/roles/jobs who might be involved in supporting a new hire in your location (see The Village #2 in the Appendix).
- ♦ How would each of the persons in the role describe, in eight words or less, how they supported a new hire/beginning teacher?

Later, ideas for how to fulfill each of those roles will be discussed. For now, establishing a solid basis for "why" and "who" of your program will make the "how" and "what" easier to define.

As you start creating or further adding to your village of people to support new teachers, think about these questions:

> How might a new hire know where to go with different questions or concerns?
> Have each team members' roles and their importance been defined and shared? Or is it an assumption that everyone knows the value and their role?

You need to identify the core values of the district/school and your program, and the critical roles to help support those values. While it may be implied that the person in the current role knows those values, having them clarified and articulated creates a system that can be sustained as roles and jobs change. Once they are defined, having a flow chart or organization resource that can be referred to can be a helpful tool. For example, if a new hire has a question about insurance, certification, curriculum, technology, or classroom management, how might they know whom their first point of contact should be?

Here are various village members to consider. Feel free to add other titles or positions that might exist in your district or region:

> *District leaders*
> *School Board*
> *Principal*
> *Instructional coach*
> *Interventionists/counselors*
> *Colleagues*
> *Community members/businesses/clubs, etc.*
> *Department/Grade level chairs*
> *Technology*
> *PTO/PTA president/members*
> *Health Services/School nurse*
> *Human Resources*
> *Custodian/Secretary/Kitchen staff*
> *Board of Education support key*
> *School Resource Officer*
> *Home/School liaisons*

Contracted staff (outside practitioners/PT/counselors)
Young professionals network
Retired teachers
Local businesses
Assistant principals
Activities/Athletic director

✅ Key Takeaway

- The village of support, comprising various individuals who may be consistently present or occasional helpers, plays a vital role in shaping the program's success.

Section 2

MAKING IT HAPPEN

4

We Have the Who, Now to the How

The people are in place and the message and *why* of supporting new hires and beginning teachers has been delivered. The village is ready to make it happen. *How* do you make it happen? Three key time segments for induction can be the guide: onboarding, orientation, and the hub of induction.

A popular chain restaurant opened a store in the largest city near us. Its arrival brought much attention…and very long lines for in-store seating and at the drive-thru. My daughter chose this restaurant as her reward for a job well done after a competition. Our time available to eat was short, yet we proceeded to merge into the drive-thru line. What happened next was nothing short of impressive. It was the quickest and most efficient drive-thru experience I ever had experienced, accompanied by friendly service that left a lasting positive impression. This major fast food restaurant drive-thru was a well-oiled, impressive, customer service oriented, chicken producing machine! From my perspective, they certainly set themselves apart in the fast food industry for efficiency and performance. Curious about how that happens and if there is anything to be learned in the education world, I began to look at their model of operation and training. What I found was worth consideration when developing our own plan for growth and development.

DOI: 10.4324/9781003487470-8

The training process for this fast food chain includes a very clear set of workforce principles and priorities. This company's employee training is thorough, customizable, and designed around the behaviors and operational aspects that really matter to customers. Each franchise owner is encouraged to put their own touches on how they train their teams based on their specific area and need. At the same time, the materials, resources, and methods supplied by the organization are of the best quality and relay the same consistent message and values. The company values are very clear, and how they carry them out reflects this. Their core values focus on service, teamwork, purpose, and innovation.

The "how" is based on their "why" and includes a well-orchestrated plan. While the corporate world is remarkably different in many ways from the education world, there are some structures and lessons that may be gleaned to contribute to progress.

How do you share and communicate what you value? Hopefully, the interview started the process of helping your new hire know what your district or building is about. Putting it into action throughout the induction process with a plan is key.

The corporate world has been developing models of introducing new employees to their companies for many years. When planning, thinking in smaller time segments can help clarify the focus for the different *parts* of the process. Dividing the time frames into sections upon hiring can help to break the planning process into smaller steps. One consideration is this division.

> When planning, thinking in smaller time segments can help clarify the focus for the different *parts* of the process.

Induction as a process described in this book includes:

- <u>Onboarding</u>: the time frame from official school board approval leading up to the first day of contract reporting which is often new hire orientation days. One might

even consider the interview process also as a time to start laying the foundation of the onboarding process by providing the essentials of understanding key elements of a school district or building.
- ♦ Orientation: the identified day(s) before school starts specifically for new hire training.
- ♦ Induction Hub: the support provided throughout the entire school year during which the "hub" or majority of sustainable support takes place following orientation.

It is semantics as to how the employee training processes and these three commonly used words are used. There is nothing particularly sacred about the labels above, only that they are defined. The words and the inferences in meaning made the most sense to the person instrumental in the planning of them (myself), so that is what stuck. Use whatever sticks for your district and those who are making the work happen. You have professional liberty to categorize them as necessary, as long as everyone involved in the work knows what they mean.

These three areas will be where specific ideas for the relivables and repeatables discussed previously can be discovered and confirmed (you already do that), or where new or even better ideas emerge.

What Are the Big Ideas around the Work?

Within the roles of onboarding, orientation, and induction, there are four key workplace components for consideration and guidance. When considering any workplace, Talya Bauer, Ph.D., author of *Onboarding New Employees: Maximizing Success*, part of the SHRM Foundation's Effective Practice Guidelines Series (Hirsch, 2017) identified these four important aspects as key features to the induction process:

- ♦ Culture: learning the unique "personality" of an organization

- Compliance: on-the-job basics needed for a given job
- Clarification: details and context of one's job
- Connection: key interpersonal relationships and support mechanisms

Keeping these four key features in mind as a foundational framework can be valuable in planning your program.

Key Takeaways

- The induction process can be divided into three main time frames: onboarding, orientation, and the hub of induction
- Culture, compliance, clarification, and connections are the 4 c's to help guide the planning of each stage.

5

All Onboard! Onboarding and Saying Hello

When the official school board approval of a new hire and contract is finalized, it is an exciting time! For our beginning teachers, their dream of teaching is starting to materialize. All of the possibilities of changing lives and beginning their career are starting to swirl around in their minds. Dreams of what they want their classroom to be like are being imagined. For others with experience, starting in a new district may mean a fresh start, new possibilities, and hopes for being their best in a new place. Building on this excitement is why onboarding should begin as soon as possible. In an ideal scenario, there are anywhere from several weeks or months between the official hiring and the start date. This step might be very quick between onboarding, orientation, and the hub of induction starting with day one of the official start to school.

As teachers embark on their official journey in the upcoming school year, it becomes crucial to extend a warm welcome. Equally important is the reassurance that safety features are in place and a seasoned crew is prepared to guide their way. As they embark upon uncharted territory, the easier the new places are to navigate, the more equipped they will be for their next steps. This is why it is important to think about their initial challenges of being new to the profession, district, and community.

DOI: 10.4324/9781003487470-9

It is time to practice the vuja de mentioned previously and consider the lens of a new person in your district. Remember, *vuja de is the practice of viewing the familiar through a fresh lens.* (You have read this before, so you are not having déjà vu.) Think about the perspective of someone new to your district. What essentials might a newcomer need to begin their journey with your team and feel integrated into the learning community? Consider how to convey a hearty welcome and share your enthusiasm for their presence. Whose voices should they hear, and when is the optimal time for them to hear from these members of the learning village?

> Onboarding as a part of induction should begin as soon as possible after hiring.

Onboarding as a part of induction should begin as soon as possible after hiring. Remember, it is a process not an event and should, if possible, begin to take place prior to the official start of the school year. Beginning to develop a relationship with the new teacher will help them to feel welcomed and generate excitement for joining the team. When a new teacher orientation is planned right before school begins, the time leading up to this event can focus on fostering the connection between the new teacher and the school or district. What is feasible and most appropriate for each district may vary. The availability of a new teacher to engage in activities or communication before the official start date will likely also vary. Resources and information need to be available at any time.

A new teacher mentor, a team within a department, a grade level of teachers, building principal, central office administration, and any other member of the village can each decide the impact they will have on welcoming a beginning teacher to the profession or a new hire to the team. Regardless of the size of the school district or role of the village member, there are certain components that can help to make a transition smoother for a new teacher. They include both education related and non-education related considerations.

If you have ever moved to a new house, town, state, or even country, the transition process can be made smoother (or more difficult) by what happens throughout the process. It is extremely helpful to have a clear destination or place to live, have the core necessities in place upon arrival (e.g., electricity and water turned on), meet people who jump in to help along the way, and have clear communication of how to get things done, whom to ask questions, or how to start the process of learning about your new surroundings. These are some possible considerations and examples of non-education related issues that can impact the start of a person's journey in your community. When you can help enhance the transition process to a new community even in small ways, the opportunity for the new hire to be able to focus on teaching and student learning will also benefit.

Ask your current people what their biggest challenges and frustrations were in getting started. They will be the best resource for learning more. Once, a teacher shared how she was looking for a place to rent and viewed a house in an alarming condition and location. This was one of her first welcomes and introductions to the community. As a result, we created a relationship with realtors and landlords to provide a more positive initial impression and experience in our community and district.

> Ask your current people what their biggest challenges and frustrations were in getting started. They will be the best resource for learning more.

On the education related side of starting new in a district, the barrage of information at the beginning of the school year can be very overwhelming. Finding ways to disseminate information in smaller chunks over time lets it sink in and be absorbed gradually, instead of it arriving all at once.

Here are a few ideas for consideration during the onboarding phase:

- Welcome phone call or email: Who would be important for the new hire to hear from? This may be one person or several people. Anyone can do it and it can mean a lot. A phone call from the building principal, superintendent, or department chair to say, "Welcome, we are excited for you to join us. What questions might I answer?" is a gesture that can go a long way. A handwritten note or an email can be sent to, too. (See Sample Welcome Letter #3 in the Appendix.) The size and makeup of your school and district can impact this decision. If you are one of five new staff members in a district or one of 2,500, there would be a different plan for this. It is like how in a very tiny town the mayor may welcome you; in a huge city you might like it if one neighbor made eye contact. Thus it may need to be a building or even department/grade level task, while in other settings the superintendent may reach out as well.

- Living accommodations: Visiting places to live is often the first impression your new hire may have of your community. What is available for housing? It is always a bonus to have employees reside in the community. Helping them find a way to do this can make the process more appealing. You can prepare a contact list of people to call as a place to start, or contact local realtors or landlords ahead of time. Having a working relationship with reputable landlords and real estate agents can go a long way in helping make the housing search much less stressful. The quality of the realtors can also impact how the new staff members view the community they are becoming a part of, so please choose wisely. We want our new hires to be treated as professionals and to feel safe and valued as a community member.

- Things to do before orientation: This can be a list of things that might be done in advance to prepare for orientation and the school year. These are only suggestions and should not be considered mandatory. It is important to remember that everyone operates differently when preparing. Some new hires will read everything repeatedly and follow each suggestion with follow-up questions, while others may not check emails until the day before arrival. Provide for both types of personalities and everything in between. (See Things to Do Before Orientation #4 in the Appendix.)

- Technology: A great way to start the welcome wagon is giving new hires a district email to begin communication and become a part of staff group emails. Providing login access and information for key programs can be a helpful tool. It was described earlier, but making sure the technology does not get in the way is truly an easy induction win for a school.
- "In Your Shoes" panel: Who knows better about what to expect than the previous new teachers? Provide an opportunity for the incoming teachers to interact with a panel of former year 1 and 2 teachers. This can easily be done using an online video conferencing format so participants can join from anywhere.
- Need-to-know information for orientation/dates, etc.: Provide location, dress code, tentative agenda, food options, and other considerations as a preview of what to plan for. Just like preparing students for standardized testing, we do not want the format of the test to interfere with the results.
- Central office info: What is the plan for the paperwork? Filling out insurance and tax information can be overwhelming, especially for those completing it for the first time. How can you help them plan for this step of the process? Is a specific date needed, or are options available online or in-person? Where do they go and who do they ask for? It is very important to have a good communication system in place and a clear understanding of the hiring process with the Human Resource department. Reducing the number of disconnect opportunities can save a lot of time and questions. When forms and paperwork are more important to the district than they are to the new hire, we need to be doubly supportive to make the event seamless and efficient when possible.
- Community resources: What resources are available in your community? A local Chamber of Commerce may be a good partner. Our local businesses provide a welcome bag with coupons and goodies. An individual school may

want to do this with the thought of businesses that are close in proximity and are located in the attendance area.
- Head start in learning: How can summer school be used to help train incoming teachers? You can have an audience of students for new hires to practice new programs being learned, or try out strategies they may have not used before. Clearly this would have to be voluntary and participants would need to be compensated, but some teachers new to teaching might appreciate the opportunity.
- Central resource location: Is there a central location online for teachers to access and find information? This can include paperwork, FAQs, video tutorials for technology, resources for learning, and anything else that is often repeated information for new hires and mentors. This can be resources of your district or school as well as links, websites, and so on. Repeatables may include:
  - Technology resources for tasks such as requesting a sub, taking attendance, entering grades, logging parent contacts, reporting technology problems, accessing building/district wide programs, etc.
  - Procedures for district wide and building technology work orders, contacts for common questions, district login info, insurance, sick leave information, reserving a school vehicle, important dates.
  - Tips for starting the school year, sample lesson plans, and other important to dos or reminders.
- Get to know the building: Is last year's yearbook available for them to look at? Could a virtual building tour be available?

The new hires may have questions of their own. Answering these questions before they are asked will show that you have planned for your new teachers and are ready to help them be successful.

These are common questions:

- Will the principal reach out to me or should I reach out to them?
- When can I get into my room?

- Who is my mentor? Should I contact them or will they contact me?
- What is the dress code?
- Do I need to attend any summer training?

Already, your new hires are learning about the 4 c's of culture, compliance, clarification, and connections available in the district. Their beginning, thanks to you, has already started working toward their success and those of your students. The new teacher is learning the culture of support awaiting them, finding out the important things they need to do to get started, getting an idea of what they need to do to be prepared, and starting to build connections with some key people to help them get started on their journey.

Key Takeaways

- Onboarding as a part of induction should begin as soon as possible after hiring.
- Considering the challenges and common steps of a new teacher new to a district and possibly new to a geographic location, make available onboarding support and resources.

6

Modeling Is Orientation

Orientation: You Have to Be What You Want to See

How do you prepare to say "Hello" in person to your newest and most important instructional leaders of your students? What do you want to see Day 1 in the classroom from the very best classroom teacher? What *you want* to see the teachers doing in their classrooms should be modeled for them when they arrive to begin their job. What better way to be what you want to see than to show them! This is a helpful mindset guide for everything you do to support new teachers. These things can be desired/expected/taught at the school or district level, but it is important that they supplement and support each other rather than conflict or contrast. Some of the possibilities of what you would want to see on Day 1 in a classroom may include:

- greeting students at the door
- providing clear expectations for learning and classroom behavior
- building a pleasant culture of learning
- working on developing connections, smiles, welcoming attitude
- creating a welcoming environment
- developing a strong classroom culture
- instilling clear routines and procedures

DOI: 10.4324/9781003487470-10

- engaging learning opportunities
- developing rapport and clear communication with parents
- being a team member of the building
- asking questions
- developing a system of organization and prioritization

Dee Ann Turner shares an insightful perspective:

> Hopefully, new staff have learned about the purpose, mission, core values and guiding principles during the selection process. Orientation is where these elements come to life for the new staff member through storytelling and experiencing the culture firsthand. Prepare to have available everything the new employee needs on Day 1. Name badges, uniforms, parking passes, office space, telephones, computers and any other tools or equipment an employee needs should be set up and ready to go on the very first day. (Turner, 2019)

> What *you want* to see the teachers doing in their classrooms should be modeled for them when they arrive to begin their job.

You have to be what you want to see.

The number of new teachers and size of a district will determine the length, agenda, and planning of orientation. While there is not a one size fits all model, there are some commonalities among many orientation programs for districts of varying sizes. Orientation also does not have to be a formal process initiated only by the district. Well-articulated plans and considerations should also be created within specific buildings and departments or grade level teams. This is the time to again model what is important, share critical information for getting started, and help the new hire to assimilate to the learning community.

The better the systems in place at the start of the year to assist newcomers, the smoother the experience for everyone involved—students, colleagues, mentors, principals, and all those who are part of the induction journey. Much like the classroom management process, time invested early in the process will pay dividends for everyone involved in the long term.

As we know, modeling is the minimum of guidance, not the maximum. We also need to share the "why" of how we make choices on greeting students as well as what to do with the various responses we might receive in return. If at every level—district, building, etc.—the same welcoming actions take place the more they are reinforced. If at the district level they are greeted and at the building level they are not, what exactly is being modeled?

> Time invested early in the process will pay dividends for everyone involved in the long term.

Once you know what you want to see from your newest teachers, there are many important next steps to consider: how will each member of the village responsible model this? What is the most important message and information to impart? Who needs to know? Who does it so well that they can be a part of the modeling process? This is where the four pillars of culture, compliance, clarification, and connection will need consideration.

Orientation Considerations

New teacher orientation is an event that has the opportunity to leave a lasting impression and set the tone for the days ahead as an employee. This may be where the relivables for your district start. A relivable is having a new hire remember at the end of the school year the details of orientation and the positive start to their school year. Each district will have its own needs and training to usher its new teachers into the learning and culture of its workplace. Regardless of the size of a district, there are a few key components to keep in mind and consider when planning for new teacher orientation.

When you travel to a new location, you may find yourself looking for some kind of a sign providing directions of where to go and what to do. Think about the first time you entered a new place such as a new city, office building, doctor's office, or hotel. You naturally want to quickly become acclimated to your surroundings. The more unsure you are about where you are or why you are there, the more anxious you may become about the unknown. Where do I go, where do I sit, who do I need to talk to, or will I have what I need? Oftentimes, the first people who greet you (or don't) and the ability to navigate your surroundings, thanks to good signage or people to assist, can leave a lasting impression on your experience there.

"What would you expect a great teacher to do when welcoming students into the classroom?" is the best guide for planning for new teacher orientation. It will be key to have a plan for the arrival of the new teachers—where to go, where to sit, greeting them, and providing activities and information to introduce them to the district, school, or team. The seemingly smaller details, such as a welcome sign to let them know they have arrived and a person to immediately help them feel welcome, can start things off on a positive trajectory. While it may not seem like a big deal to the people planning, it can make a difference to a nervous new teacher.

Does your district/school/team value teamwork and collaboration? Plan activities to model this. Does the district/school/team value its employees getting to know the students and forming relationships—it will be important for this to happen at orientation, too. Again, you have to be what you want to see. Modeling is not just for teachers to do with students. It is important to pass the message of importance along by demonstrating it. Talk the talk while walking the walk.

Possible ideas for orientation may include:

- opportunities to get to know one another
- meet district administrators and key people for support at each level
- necessary learning and training needed, district and building most important information (Can this be done in an engaging way?)
- model classroom experience
- tour of school/district buildings—especially those most relevant to new staff members
- tour of community/introduction to businesses
- time in buildings for building specific learning

- time in classrooms to work
- work time one-on-one with mentors
- good food, well fed people are usually happy
- a glimpse into the district and/or school culture
- online possibilities to front load information prior to face-to-face—or enhance face-to-face by sharing less significant information in a different format
- personalization of large groups by creating smaller groups

Here are some more detailed examples of what some schools may include in orientation to capture the culture, compliance, clarification, and connection throughout the orientation process. This is a place where relivables and many repeatables may exist:

<u>Delivering important district information</u>: There is important information that needs to be communicated from a district level. This can vary from a welcome message delivered by key district leaders to the compliance and clarification details that have implications. Important information may lend itself to delivery in a direct manner for which listeners "sit and get" or sit and listen to the speaker. There is nothing wrong with direct instruction when done well. What does "done well" look like? Keeping it short, simple (to the point), and with stories usually helps. Another consideration is finding engaging ways, such as a scavenger hunt, cooperative learning structures, or other creative ways, to help deliver important information with a spark. It also helps to have the most engaging central office people do the majority of the delivery if possible. The same is true at the building level.

A few examples of what a district can do for orientation include friendly competition and fun. For example, we did a digital scavenger hunt app. The different school teams, led by the building administrators, completed tasks and learned at stations throughout the downtown area. Central office administrators were a part of the stations in different locations and had the opportunity to visit with small groups throughout the morning. Many downtown/local merchants welcomed the new hires in different ways, from signs, to standing on the sidewalks to greet them, and offering samples of the food at their restaurants. Our new hires learned about our public library, community theater, park department, and many other features of our retail area, while also learning about the school district. A little friendly competition and picture opportunities added an extra element of fun. We have also stayed within our campus and created stations in a school building. Principals and their new teacher team traveled to different rooms to learn from district employees such as the superintendents, school nurse, and technology support team. This was another way for orientation to have an interactive spin. Local civic organizations have provided lunch in the park, or food trucks with yard games which were a great opportunity for fun and culture building during orientation. While this might not work for a large group with big numbers, in a smaller setting of buildings or departments, a creative spin on needed information can still happen. In larger districts, these might work at the building level. Finding ways to adapt or spark new ideas is how a planning team can really gain momentum.

Districts and individual buildings could also have buses take new staff around to get a sense of the dynamics of where students reside. They could also get lunch, snacks, and desserts at some of the local eateries while touring. These things could also be done at any time of year as it might be enlightening to see the background of the students and increase an understanding of the challenges and dynamics they face daily.

Key initiatives: What are the basics of training for getting started in any key initiatives or programs to be implemented? Consider the top three to five essentials a new hire needs to know and begin to implement them on day one in the classroom or the first few weeks of school. Help the other educators (fellow team teachers, grade level partners, etc.) who will be working closest with the new teacher to remember their newness in the journey. It is easy to play the comparison game when learning something new. A new hire might become frustrated when those who are further along on the implementation journey make it look easy. Later during the hub of the induction process, it will be important to provide further training and revisit these key essentials once the school year and actual implementation has begun.

Remember to balance those at each level so the new teachers are not overwhelmed and also seem to have a logical fit with each level. Consider curriculum and technology training or support. How will this be provided and what will be the most important starting out?

Model classroom: This is an opportunity for your most outstanding teachers to provide modeling. This can be at a district wide level where the new teachers gather to learn. This process can also be done at a building, department, or grade level to meet more specific needs. A model classroom can include from start to finish examples of what a day in a classroom might look like. You could choose from multiple outstanding teachers to model a variety of effective teaching practices. These might include common procedures, a day in the life of a student, technology learning, starting and end of day routines, and anything else that would be helpful to know and see before students arrive. (See Model Classroom Guide Example #5 in the Appendix.)

Voices of teachers: One way to consider easing some of the nervousness that goes with arriving at a new place is to make available and hear from current teachers. Recruit some of your "best" to be the faces of the district from the get-go. Let them welcome, share, model, and shine their light for those coming in.

Differentiation opportunities: As you plan orientation and the next step of onboarding, give special consideration to varying routes of certification and experience. Some new hires may be experienced teachers while others are the newest teachers to the profession. Beginning teachers who have completed a four-year degree program and student teaching experience most likely have different needs than the newest teachers who are on an emergency or alternate certification track. These teachers may need extra intensive support to help them get off to a strong start and maintain it throughout the year. Consider ramping up those support systems for specific needs such as specific content instruction and strategies, more detailed classroom management support, special education training, and the basics of lesson planning, grading, documentation, use of technology for learning, and the underlying "why" of each of these. The size of the district would certainly determine the availability and timing of orientations. A combination of in-person and synchronous and asynchronous training may be options for consideration.

Time to apply what they have learned: Orientation can feel like the first of many drinking from a fire hose moments. So much information to absorb at once can be overwhelming. It can be helpful to find time for new hires to return to their classrooms to apply what they have learned. Help them to practice organization and prioritizing skills by supporting goal setting for what they hope to accomplish when returning to the classroom to work. This is a time they can also further explore the repeatable resources to review what they learned or possibly seek the answer to a question they may have.

Mentor training and time with their mentee: The role of a mentor is critical in supporting a beginning teacher. Even an experienced teacher as a new hire needs a person or buddy to serve as a resource. Allow scheduled time to meet and provide training for mentors. Each district may do this differently from training prior to the school year, online, or in another format. Consider having the mentor attend with their mentee at the beginning of the year meetings with the principal during orientation. Have both the mentee and mentor hear the same information to maintain consistency in information. More ideas and resources for supporting mentors will be shared later.

Learning about the community: There are many ways to introduce your newest people to the community in which their students live. By learning about the community in which they are serving, a new hire can have a better understanding of the culture and demographics of their students and those factors that may impact student learning. As mentioned earlier, a school bus ride tour through neighborhoods not only sheds some light on the community from which students come, but also reminds adults what riding on a school bus can feel like. For example, if it is a hot August day, a school bus ride can impact the mood of its rider before ever arriving at school. To further make connections between buildings and its leaders, you can use the bus trip as an opportunity to connect the principals' faces to their buildings. At each school building where the principal(s) works, they can hop on the bus to share a "fun fact" about a district wide procedure, such as reserving a school vehicle for travel, a text alert system for school closure, and other important information. Your local Chamber of Commerce or community outreach organization may be a great partner on a tour of the community in highlighting key features of the surrounding community. Sometimes knowing where to get a car fixed, buy groceries, or enjoy an activity is important information. Orientation should be fun, engaging, and a learning opportunity.

Enlist the students, community, or other teachers: Motivating and bringing the "hype" have been a fun way for some districts to welcome their teachers, both new and returning. Who better to lay out the red carpet for welcoming than the cheerleaders or band members displaying their talents? The high school cheerleaders, band, or students in general have been used as a welcoming crew to cheer and usher in the educators to the building or meetings. Maybe a community group hosts tables or provides a meal to show their support and greet the new hires.

See the faces of district or building personnel: In districts both large and small, knowing who you are reaching out to for questions and putting a name and face together can be helpful. Find ways to connect names and faces to people for whom a new hire may be interacting to create a smaller sense of community.

- ♦ Building specific support: Within buildings, there are often people who come and go who may never be introduced. Yet these people can be as critical to the success of a teacher. Custodial/maintenance staff, health care workers, school nurse, and school couriers might be a few to consider providing introductions to.

Peek into the evaluation process: The evaluation process can be a mysterious and seemingly frightening dark cloud hanging over the heads of beginning or experienced teachers. The truth is they worry a lot about getting fired when starting a new job. Too much information about the evaluation process before school starts can be overwhelming, yet no information about the process can be equally as scary. During orientation when the mentor and mentee are both available to hear the information is a great time to briefly cover the highlights of the process. More details can be shared later as the induction process unfolds. This is often a big concern for beginning teachers.

The evaluation process is an example of how the district as a whole and all building leaders must be connected. At the building level, the processes and structures can be shared, but if they are actually evaluated at the individual school site, the principals, assistants, and evaluators are the ones that need to communicate their methods and expectations. It is nice to read about something like this in a manual, but it is essential to hear it from the actual assessors. Evaluation is also something that does not have to be shared before a person starts teaching. However, it must be shared before a person will be evaluated. We all want to know the rules of the game before the game begins.

Supplies for getting started: The excitement of a new classroom is a much-anticipated part of the new job; a place to make your mark with the decorations you have planned or put one's own touch to the space. It is disheartening to walk into a room that was left a mess and nothing needed can be found. One idea is to have a department/grade level leader in charge of a supply box. The exiting teacher from the previous year should be responsible for placing all manuals, remotes, digital devices, and school purchased supplies in a designated box or container so it is readily available for the new teacher. Have the team leader or department chair check and be in charge of the box to ensure the next teacher has what they need. A checklist of these items would also be helpful to ensure consistency among rooms for each new hire in a building. It is so much more professional and reassuring to walk into a new setting that is ready to go than it is for someone new to waste precious time looking for something they have no idea where it should be found.

Walk and learn: With an experienced educator, take a ghost walk through classrooms before school starts or after school. A ghost walk is a walk into empty classrooms that are set up for the school to begin. Use this as an opportunity to look at different seating arrangements and organization of materials. It is an opportunity to discuss transitions where students are moving, opportunities for teachers to use proximity with students and circulate a classroom, as well as organization strategies that might be important for classroom management procedures (Kachur et al., 2013, 81–82).

Whatever is on your list, you must consider what is in place to clearly communicate what is most important. What will you provide in training, support, and resources to optimize the opportunity for the learning to happen? Out of all these, what are the priorities for a beginning teacher starting out? Everything seems important and that can be very overwhelming.

The new hires may have questions of their own. Answering these questions before they are asked will show that you have planned for your new teacher and are ready to help them be successful. These are common questions:

- Where do I park?
- Where do I go when I arrive at the orientation location?
- Do we have name tags?
- Do we have assigned seats?
- Where do I sit when walking into a room full of people?
- Am I going to have to talk to a room full of people?
- What should I wear to orientation?
- Will I be asked if I have any dietary restrictions for food?
- I keep hearing acronyms. Where can I find out what they mean? (Provide a place to look them up or a page with them listed.)
- How am I going to remember everyone's name?
- Who does a person go to in the team, building, or district for specific questions?
- I have no idea where to start, what do I do with information I've received, or what do I do next? Who can help me?
- Can anyone tell I'm nervous?

Other times, the new teacher may feel so overwhelmed by all the new learning, they are not sure what questions to ask. Provide a list of questions (see New Teacher Questions #6 in the Appendix) for them to consider asking so they have less work trying to figure out what information they need the most and so you can ensure nothing has been overlooked.

By now, new teachers should have experienced some of the culture of your district or building. The focus of the learning during this time helps to provide that insight. Compliance to district and building expectations should have been discussed and resources provided to revisit and access this information again. Clarification of the new teacher's job through mentor and principal conversations and work are bringing into focus the plan for the start of the school year. Connections with colleagues and others in the district have begun to form. The advancement to the starting line of the school year has arrived.

Key Takeaways

- The better the systems in place at the start of the year to assist newcomers, the smoother the experience for everyone involved—students, colleagues, mentors, principals, and all those who are part of the induction journey.
- Whatever is important to see the teachers doing in their classrooms should be modeled for them when they arrive at orientation.

7

The Hub of Induction

How do we keep the momentum of the first weeks of school going when enthusiasm and hope are high? After the newness of the school year wears off and the reality of teaching sets in, how will the teachers continue to be supported? Induction as a support process is the big picture of supporting new teachers throughout the entire year, as well as beyond the first year of teaching. It includes onboarding and orientation, the start of the school year, and extends to the end of the school year and even beyond to the next years. Many of the ideas should continue into the following year or years in scaffolding support. After the onboarding and orientation process, the main "hub" of induction will take place. A hub by definition is the central location and where the most activity takes place (*Cambridge English Dictionary: Definitions & Meanings*, n.d.). This reference will be used to distinguish between induction as a process and the hub of the induction period starting after orientation until the end of the school year. Another way to think of this stage is a marathon race as compared to smaller sprints of onboarding and orientation.

The induction hub, which needs very intentional planning, can be the most important and yet most challenging part of the support process. It is a time when new teachers are most likely to make a shift from seeing themselves as ready for the challenge, to adopting a survival mode, especially during the first year (Thomas & Beauchamp, 2011).

DOI: 10.4324/9781003487470-11

The New Teacher Center and founder Ellen Moir (1990), identified four common stages of a first-year teacher. Although not every novice teacher follows this precise sequence, these phases offer valuable insights to all involved in supporting new educators and providing a general understanding of potential hurdles. Knowing these generalized potential stages and planning for support and check-in opportunities will be important. Throughout an academic year, educators progress through several stages—starting from anticipation, moving to survival, experiencing disillusionment, seeking rejuvenation, embracing reflection, and ultimately circling back to anticipation.

When considering the learning opportunities, the needs of the beginning teachers are likely different from those with experience. When working on the hub of induction, keep in mind the common challenges that may be occurring at the beginning, middle, or toward the end of a school year. Keep in mind that certain times of the school year offer different events, situations, and challenges. Refer back to the beginning teacher stages to provide insight of challenges to consider when planning. Beginning teacher learning should also provide plenty of opportunities to collaborate (and commiserate) with other beginning teachers, as well as high quality experienced teachers when appropriate and if possible. A sense of not being alone in the struggles helps to reassure a beginning teacher that they are not unique in their challenges. The opportunities to facilitate a sense of camaraderie can take place within buildings, districts, regions, or even digitally.

Another reason planning for the hub stage of induction is important is the reality that once school starts, it is easy for even the important things to get overlooked. Mentors who are classroom teachers have their own classrooms to run and students to teach. A building principal has many parts of their job requiring their attention. This is not to suggest that anyone intentionally forgets a new hire or beginning teacher. It is the nature of a busy school day, week, and month. Juggling many balls in the air means a few may get dropped. This is the reason an articulated plan needs to be in place ahead of starting this phase. The more meticulous the planning, the less likely it becomes for any essential aspects to go unnoticed. Keep in mind the 4 c's of connection, compliance, clarification, and connection throughout the process to ensure the wheels of induction keep rolling forward toward progress.

So where does the person(s) tasked with building the yearlong and beyond induction hub begin? How does a district, school, or team plan to keep the induction wheels rolling forward once orientation is over?

These general areas and key features of induction hub planning to support new teachers throughout the year can help provide a framework. Ideas to provide support and growth for new educators are numerous and can fit districts and schools of all sizes. When considering the induction hub, choose one or two areas to begin building upon or expanding:

- planned professional learning opportunities
- planned support and check ins
- support for/in the classroom work (classroom management, lesson planning, and instruction/student learning)
- support for emotional/social development
- support for mentors
- celebrations

Building a structure on sand will only yield short-term usability. A sturdy foundation is needed for long-term results. Just as a strong foundation is vital for a structure's purpose and stability, a classroom strategy's effectiveness hinges on its underlying purpose. The "why" behind its implementation is as important as the intended outcome. Integrate support components into the induction hub, and understand the rationale behind what you choose to support and reinforce in the hub. Even if you're introducing just a couple of ideas to fortify support for new teachers, the clarity of purpose and the commitment to sustaining these are key. True improvement takes root and endures when these aspects are clear to all involved.

To keep the strength and growth of your program strong, consider these questions to help further clarify and strengthen the foundational components:

- Providing a common district wide definition of effective teaching: How do we (as the administrators/mentors/support team) know what effective teaching looks, sounds, and feels like?
- Embracing meaningful discussion and collaboration about teaching practices: How do we determine if they are effective? Identifying and emphasizing strategies that have the greatest impact on student learning: What is most important that we would like to see teachers implementing or focusing on? Why do we consider this important?
- Focusing on continuous growth for all teachers: What is already in place that is working? What might be needed?
- Considering the various tracks of learning teachers might need: Certified teachers vs. temporary certified, regular ed classroom vs. special education, Fine Arts/Exploratory classes, etc.
- What is a time frame we can reasonably support—one year, two years, three years, beyond?

While you are planning your induction hub supports, it is critical to find the balance between support structures that truly make a new teacher's job better and the ones that add to their plates creating more stress. If you ask them to leave their classroom for professional development, help them to plan in advance for this, and select who will be covering their classroom. If you ask them to read an article or do a book study, give them enough time to do this, or choose other tasks that they can do in its place. If they are asked to give up a planning period for a discussion or meeting, provide plenty of advance notice or another opportunity to have their work time in the day, which shows consideration for their already busy schedule. Some expectations come with being a professional, and learning to manage time and responsibilities is a part of the learning process. This might also be a skill to consider supporting or helping to learn as a part of the induction hub professional learning. Consider the time, planning, and long-term impact of each induction component before starting.

The following are some induction hub components for consideration.

Key Components to Consider When Inducting New Teachers

1. <u>Planned and timely professional learning opportunities</u>: Classroom management, lesson planning, and instruction for student learning were the three main pillars for the planning and continuous revision of our new teacher induction program for beginning teachers' professional learning opportunities. These are also very broad areas subject to interpretation. One or even ten magic formulas or strategies for being successful at any of these do not exist but thousands of resources for the many ways to do them are available. Several factors determine the success for which each is carried out. Yet, there are also some key principles that seem to be sticking points for each. For example, we know that routines and procedures in place, practiced, and reinforced are foundational to strong classroom management. Instruction that is engaging, well-planned, and focused on learning standards and student learning is critical. Regardless which program, philosophy, or framework a district may use, planning for ways to support the growth of the common truths of teaching are the focus of the induction hub. These are some basic principles that guide decisions for choosing the strategies for teachers to try or people to share. These might be a few for consideration as you think about what is most important for sharing thinking and strategies with new hires:

- Are students learning? How do we know?
- Are students engaged in learning? How do we know?
- Are these the most effective use of time to meet learning standards?
- How is the classroom community welcoming to all students?
- Are resources available for struggling and accelerated learners?

Every school district has a teacher evaluation process designed to help its educators grow in practice and identify underperforming teachers to provide support for improvement. This process should be based on very clear expectations and understanding of what a district and administrator consider to be effective. We ask teachers to use their curriculum for student growth, and we should too for teacher growth. Once again, we refer back to the thinking we expect our teachers to use, learn, and develop. Students (and in this case teachers) at all levels need to continue to grow, learn, and improve with support from their leadership. Professional learning or development is the common way we do this in education. Consider the important roles that both central office and individual buildings must provide in this process.

Professional learning can take many different forms. As technology has evolved, the opportunity for the most relevant learning moments has become even more personalized based on needs.

Here are a few examples of what professional learning opportunities for new hires might be:

- Observing other teachers. This should include a clear focus or purpose prior to the observation along with, and a process for, pre and post observation conversations and reflection.
- Reflection opportunities (discussed more in-depth later)
- After school and during the day professional learning days/development with timely and specific focuses
- Access to library of resources or subscriptions to professional development resources
- Instructional coaches/coaching cycles
- All staff/building presenters, coaches, workshops, etc.
- Mentoring of planned and unplanned learning moments
- Learning walks
- Self-guided learning-podcasts, online groups, webinars
- Book study/small group work
- Teacher learning/hands-on training in the summer during summer school

Just as one might expect a teacher to know his or her learners and developmental levels when planning, the same is true with professional learning for our newest educators. Surveys, classroom observations, conversations, and student needs will help guide decisions for all group learning, small group learning, and individualized learning opportunities for the teachers. Having follow-up surveys and support ensures the new teachers' needs are being met and growth opportunities are being implemented.

Implementation planning is also key for thinking about. The entry point for which teachers are able to learn something new and return to their classroom and implement it can vary greatly depending on the teacher, the content, and the support available. Being realistic about what a beginning teacher versus an experienced teacher can be expected to do, know, and implement needs consideration. At a curriculum workshop I attended, a model curriculum was shared with many hands-on, critical thinking components. It was exactly what one would hope to see for learning in a classroom. An experienced principal spoke up and shared that while this was excellent learning for students and great ideas, the reality of a first-year teacher being able to implement something so robust needed consideration. Cooperative learning activities, hands-on activities, and all things engaging take organization and strong classroom management skills to execute with success. There are beginning teachers who can handle all of these things. They can implement with students' great instruction strategies and learning opportunities that are hands-on, minds-on ideas. Also, it is important to recognize that common beginning teacher struggles include classroom management and organizational skills. Just because you want them to do highly engaging, critical thinking activities and you may even provide the ideas or tools to implement, it doesn't guarantee success. In fact, it could lead to more frustration if they do not feel equipped and have the support to implement. Planning for how to help the varying levels of teacher skills and giving them the tools and knowledge to scaffold their progress will be important.

> Being realistic about what a beginning teacher versus an experienced teacher can be expected to do, know, and implement needs consideration.

2. <u>Resource library</u>: This is a common thread throughout all stages of the induction process—onboarding, orientation, and the hub of induction. There are frequently questions asked by new hires each year. Other times there are questions only a few will ask yet may be a common worry that others have but won't ask. New hires are often worried about bothering their colleagues with a lot of questions. Or questions may need to be answered during times for which no one else is available such as when they are no longer at school or in the early or late hours of the day. A digital resource library or some other type of resource tool to reference can be a great support to have. New hires should know how to use the student information system for its many purposes, how to request a substitute teacher in the event of a needed absence, what do the acronyms mean that I keep hearing, what are examples of professionalism, where to find paperwork, and "what to do if" kind of questions. Have a resource available at any time to show that a district prioritizes supporting a new hire by working to eliminate barriers that might prevent them from being their best. Creating short (no more than 5 minutes) video tutorials by in-district personnel can also help a new hire connect with a local district human resource and is much more inviting to listen to when you have a relevant connection.

Having someone who can curate effective videos, articles, and podcasts about effective teaching, being the new teacher, work/life balance, etc. can be of great value to new and all staff members. Of course they can always independently search online, but having a starting point they can tap into is a wonderful support for teachers.

Key Takeaways

- ♦ The induction hub includes the common challenges of new teachers at different times throughout a school year, the role of mentors, the importance of professional development opportunities, and ways to provide many resources of support.

- Consider the general areas and key features of induction hub planning to support new hires to help provide a framework. Choose one or two areas to begin building upon or expanding.
- While you are planning your induction hub supports, it is critical to find the balance between support structures that truly make a new teacher's job better and the ones that add to their plates creating more stress.

8

Learning by Observing

When observing a duck glide across the water gracefully, it may look effortless. However, what is not visible from above the water is how the duck's feet are paddling furiously beneath the water's surface. Similarly, when listening to a beautiful orchestra performance, one can appreciate the harmonious sound without necessarily grasping the role each instrument and musician play in creating it. Likewise, in a classroom, a master teacher's effective instruction involves numerous subtle actions that impact classroom management and student learning. These too, may go unnoticed by an observer. The small yet influential details such as strategic positioning while interacting with students, appropriate voice level and tone, nonverbal cues, and specific actions or words that redirect unfocused learners can make a substantial difference in classroom management and student achievement.

> A master teacher's effective instruction involves numerous subtle actions that impact classroom management and student learning.

Observation Opportunities

To support our aspiring teachers in understanding and progressing towards mastery, we must find ways to reveal the hidden

DOI: 10.4324/9781003487470-12

workings of a duck's feet beneath the water, the expertise of individual instrument sections in an orchestra, and the intricate science and art of teaching. How can we achieve this? Watching oneself and others at work in the classroom can be some of the most powerful learning opportunities available. Live action learning by watching a colleague or watching a video clip of oneself in action can provide insight and perspective that might not otherwise be seen. Three ways to do this include a classroom observation opportunity, learning walks, and self-video opportunities.

To be most effective, these observations need to be planned, purposeful, and followed by a reflective opportunity. Prior to an observation, a pre-observation conversation and goal should be established. (See Observation Goal Sheet #7 in the Appendix.) Observing another teacher or oneself without a purpose can be like traveling down the highway without a destination in mind. You may see some things that look interesting, but without an end location in mind, all the roads seem both important or unimportant. With a purpose in mind, knowing whom to watch or what to specifically watch for can make the opportunity most useful. Following the observation, a reflective conversation or opportunity to consider implications for one's own classroom makes it a valuable experience. Anytime a second person, such as an instructional coach, principal, or colleague, can be a part of any or all three phases of the observation process, this only solidifies the power of the experience in professional growth and learning.

Please consider that if we would like a teacher to observe a colleague regarding classroom management, we might want to make sure they go to the best teachers' classrooms early in the year. That is when the best teacher classroom management approaches are most visible. After a period of time, they become embedded, and rather than understanding all of the effort and thought they put into establishing the dynamic in their room, it might be easy to think they just got lucky with the students they were assigned.

Key components of observations of all kinds include:

- Intentional focus: They have a specific look while in classrooms (ex. positive language, procedures, academic vocabulary).
- Non-evaluative: These visits are for learning from others, not evaluating. Recognizing that at any given moment a classroom could have a challenge and have realistic opportunities is the goal. A super important point to emphasize is that these visits are not meant to be evaluative which can sometimes seem confusing. For example, a new teacher might be inclined to follow an observation with the good and not so good things they saw in the classroom without much context. They may have an idea of how it could be better. This is evaluative. Consideration for language in discussing the observation will be important. Providing examples of post-reflection summaries can be helpful, along with sentence stems to use when processing the experience. (See Appendix Observation Goal Sheet #7.) Instead, we would like for them to go into an observation curious. When they see something they thought was "good," wondering how a teacher is able to do that in their classroom and what skills and planning it takes to make that happen is the thinking and learning that promotes growth. Equally, if there is something the observer would consider a challenge or less desirable in a classroom, instead of going to a position of judgment, they should consider preemptive factors, as well as unknown information they may be missing.
- Pre- and post-observation briefing/debriefing: During pre-briefing, establish a reminder of the focus, time frame, and role in the classroom as an observer. Post-observation, use practiced language to discuss the learning and observations, and ask effective questions to prompt the best discussions. If a student completes a worksheet, hands it in, and receives a grade on it, is that where the learning starts and ends? If instead, they had to reflect and share with another person what they learned from the worksheet and what their next steps might be for learning, would this be more effective for both the student and the

teacher or peer? Most likely it would be. That same consideration needs to be kept in mind after any classroom observation or video reflection occurs. The opportunity to discuss and process what was noticed will always elevate the experience and learning. The reality of the school world and all of the moments and things that happened in a day might make this an easy step to skip. If we are lucky, the teacher will reflect and grow on their own, provided the opportunity to watch themself, students, and other educators.

Classroom Observation

A classroom observation alone as a single observer or along with a support person would take place in a predetermined classroom. It might be a mentor's classroom, fellow content area, or grade level teacher, or perhaps another purpose was established for the observation. There is not a magic time limit for an observation. Most important is the purpose of the observation and the opportunity to reflect following it. In the event that scheduling an in-person classroom visit is not possible, use video to record a classroom and then watch it later.

One example is "ghost" walks which could occur even before school begins. Walking through classroom set ups, but with no students to see seating arrangements and organization strategies for awareness and discussion is one way to begin the school year (Kachur et al., 2013, 81–82).

Another idea shared by Jim Knight on his instructional coaching blog (Knight, 2023) is the scenario where a coach/mentor/administrator teaches a lesson in the observer's own classroom and the teacher watches only the students. The goal of this is to help a teacher try to understand the students' emotions and needs of their students and reflect upon that.

Learning Walks
The heart of this opportunity is for teachers to visit other classrooms as a group to observe students and teachers in a classroom

setting other than their own. A group discussion follows this experience and the power of collaboration and professional dialogue further enhances the experience and learning. There are many different names for the process of learning walks and how they are structured.

Learning walks are designed to provide a focused opportunity for glimpses at the many ways learning can happen and teaching can occur, and a collaborative setting to reflect upon them. There are several ways these can happen and the logistics are mostly dependent on individual buildings. In addition to the common components of general observations, these are important additions to learning walks:

- Short visits: Visits to classrooms are short, ranging from 5 to 15 minutes. The goal is to visit several classrooms during one session if possible.
- Leadership guides the process: As a leader facilitating learning walks, ensure that clear communication about the purpose of the learning opportunity and the steps throughout are very transparent and clear to everyone involved. There should not be any surprises or gotcha's to host teachers or those observing. A person familiar with the process (ex. building administrator, instructional coach, mentor) should always accompany the groups visiting classrooms.

Video

The use of self-video is an extremely valuable tool and strategy for supporting reflective practice and thinking. Getting a clear picture of reality can best be delivered through asking a teacher to watch a video of their classroom and themselves teaching. This includes watching their students. Admittedly, it may not always be the easiest or most popular option because not everyone is comfortable seeing themselves on video. It does lend itself to vulnerability which needs to be taken into account. One way to consider this is by not requiring the teacher to share the video with anyone else the first few times or making it optional.

Also important with self-video learning is providing a clear focus when watching the video. It is easy for the person watching to get hypervigilant about noticing the sound of their voice, what they are wearing, or their body image—the things that likely won't have the biggest impact on student learning. Provide a guide to help them notice what is most important and the opportunity to gain the most from the experience. Jim Knight (2018) describes the powerful impact of video for professional growth. The opportunity to provide a clear reality picture for the person watching can greatly impact growth when done well.

Another consideration with video opportunities is logistical. It will be important to make sure the tools needed to capture the video are readily available and easy to set up. Some teachers may prefer to use their cell phone. Are there adaptable tripods or recording stands for them to use in order to set their phone in the best location? If they prefer to not use their phone, what is readily available and charged for recording? Is there an option for having someone do the recording for them? If the video has to be shared, how can this be done efficiently? Are directions available to follow? There is nothing more frustrating than spending time trying to figure out how to send a large video file.

The final considerations regarding the use of video are time and examples. We are programmed to have a limited attention span for videos. The average online videos are less than 5 minutes. A teacher can learn a lot about their classroom from watching short segments. Consider building up the process of video recording by asking them in the beginning to capture 1–2 minute segments. It can be a less formal process where they only need to have a conversation about their notices. As they become more comfortable with recording and watching, they can go deeper into the watching and learning with longer sessions and more in-depth guides. If this is a valued tool for growth and reflection, it might be important for a building administrator, instructional coach, mentor, or superintendent to

> Nothing speaks louder than walking the walk by modeling.

also consider using the same process for their learning. Nothing speaks louder than walking the walk by modeling.

Professional Learning Meetings/Workshops

Time is a valuable commodity. There never seems to be enough to get all the necessary things done. When we ask an educator to spend time in professional learning, we certainly want it to be a valuable and impactful opportunity. A person who has been in education for any amount of time can likely list what makes a professional development session worthwhile. Those factors might include gaining new ideas and practical applications for classroom instruction and student learning, time-saving tips, an enjoyable atmosphere, and the opportunity to learn with and from other like-minded professionals. Regardless if the time is being spent after school, during a school day, during a holiday break learning, and in-person or online, we want it to be valuable. This takes planning. Go to a few poorly done PD sessions and you will quickly learn what not to do for adult learners. Here are some important considerations and ideas for professional learning opportunities:

- ◆ Provide plenty of advance notice in multiple ways, multiple times. Reduce confusion or questions regarding location, times, appropriate attire, materials needed, etc. by communicating the information ahead of time more than once.
- ◆ Food is always a bonus.
- ◆ Clear focus and targets for learning are shared and revisited.
- ◆ Keep the information and focus on small chunks of learning at a time.
- ◆ Be what you want to see; plan and implement a PD session as a model for teachers to consider for their own classrooms. The goal is to find memorable ways to make the learning stick. Opportunities for discussion, movement, choices, and creativity are important if you would

like to see the same from them in their own classroom. Written, visual, and audio learning opportunities help to reach all learners.
- Be organized to establish credibility.
- Have credible information and resources/presenters.
- There's the opportunity for planning the application to their own instruction.
- Follow-up discussion and accountability opportunities show the learning time was valued.
- Consider the time of day and plan accordingly. After school learning means tired teachers will be attending, so serve them a good snack and lots of opportunities to talk. During school learning means substitute plans may need to be made and this can be stressful. Recognize and respond to the challenges each situation may present.

What might be some topics or ideas for beginning teacher professional learning? Just as a classroom teacher should spend time building community, this should also happen at the beginning of every learning session. Spending a few minutes creating connections will foster conversations later. It is also a great way to model new ideas to try in the classroom. While the topics for learning can be numerous, here are a few for consideration:

- Classroom management and behavior management scenarios and strategies
- A panel of experienced teachers for a Q&A session
- Modeling instructional strategies to implement the learning presented. For example, have teachers participate in cooperative learning structures as a way to both experience a strategy and learn while doing so.
- Experiential learning opportunities to transfer to the classroom. For example, if learning about feedback, provide an activity where teachers practice giving feedback in a different scenario.
- Common topics for most grade levels include: lesson planning, grading practices and tips, curriculum guidance, questioning strategies, assessment, vocabulary

work, cooperative learning, common classroom challenges, non-fiction reading strategies, community building, family communication, edu-tech resources.

One example of a valuable learning opportunity for new teacher support is a session to prepare for the annual family/teacher conferences. Navigating this process can be stress inducing for many beginning teachers. The timing of them may occur at about the same time as grades due for the first time, the year is in full swing, behaviors may have reared their ugly head, and life is just stressful. Meeting with parents isn't something that is usually taught in a degree program. The following chapter will provide an example of providing learning support around home communication.

Key Takeaways

- Watching oneself and others at work in the classroom can be some of the most powerful learning opportunities available.
- There are several ways for new teachers to learn by observing in other classrooms.
- A clear purpose and opportunity to reflect upon observation experience are important.

9

Peripherals Are Essential

The core of success for new teachers is essentially found in the success of their students. This is grounded in effective instruction. A car has an engine that powers its trajectory, but you also need wheels, transmission, steering mechanism, brakes, etc. to fully use the car for travel. Like the power of the engine, quality instruction is key, but there are also elements that surround instruction that can increase the chances of success for new teachers. New employees need to have guidance and conversations about essential skills that will enhance the instruction they are delivering. This chapter will explore the importance of several aspects of communication and the foundational need for the development of a solid classroom management plan. This chapter will also address how to create regular opportunities for reflection with feedback, developing organizational skills, and understanding support systems within the organization. The following content will serve as a reminder that there are important elements that surround the "engine" of a successful classroom.

Practice/Mock Family-Teacher Conferences and Contacts

Positive communication and an open, honest connection with the family of students is heralded as a key component of successful education practice. While few would argue that this is not

DOI: 10.4324/9781003487470-13

important, it is not necessarily a skill that beginning teachers (or experienced, as well) come equipped with. Sometimes the value of this communication is not well understood unless it is a priority of a team or building or if challenges that could be prevented have happened. My experience has shown it is downright terrifying for many teachers to reach out to families of students. Not knowing what to say, fear of not having an answer or being able to predict a response are common hurdles. It may also be difficult for a teacher to relate to the roles in the families of their students or understand a situation or life from their perspective. Anyone who has spent a minute in the education world knows that home to school connections can be a maze of situations, protocols, and necessary steps to navigate. This is why it will be important for the new teacher to have a clear understanding and resources regarding the expectations for home to school communication.

What are the expectations for home/school communication?

- communication prior to school starting, start and end of grade sessions
- at an Open House
- formats: newsletters/website/emails/weekly send home folders
- positive news
- academic/behavior concerns
- how often
- documentations of contacts and the importance of them

Resources to do this:

- Scripts to guide a conversation or for ideas of language to use, cite online resources
- Sitting in with other teachers/administrators for parent phone calls to listen/learn, as well as have support for conversations
- Mock parent teacher conferences with different situations (see Parent Teacher/Guardian Conference Scenarios #8 in the Appendix)

- A location to make phone calls privately and not from personal phones
- Guidance on non-verbal communication of establishing rapport, how to have difficult conversations, legal considerations
- Arrangements for in-person or virtual meetings

In the Classroom Work/Support/Day-to-Day Work and Learning
Learning opportunities are needed to grow, and implementation of the learning is needed for results. Ideas form and the learning takes place in the mind. The action has to take place in the classroom, so classroom management, lesson planning, and instruction/student learning are important. Providing support for the classroom work can happen in big and small ways. Starting to prepare ahead of the school year to provide real time support in the classroom offers many options for doing so. The range of additional classroom support can vary and needs consideration. On an easy-to-implement level, yet very helpful, is providing support for a beginning teacher, such as offering to make copies, run an errand, sort papers, cover a class for a restroom break, take over an extra school duty, such as recess, hallway, or other supervision requirement to allow more time to do what is needed. These are all very helpful during overwhelming and busy times that often occur at the beginning of the year, around report card time, holidays, and any other additional events that might be occurring. Other types of support are at a higher level of intensity and require more planning and possibly the use of additional resources.

Here are more ideas for consideration that range from easy to implement to those that take more time and planning.

<u>Classroom management plan</u>: Well-implemented routines and procedures are hailed as critical components of effective classroom management. A written classroom management plan can help new teachers consider procedures they may not have thought about or needed until the moment comes in the classroom when they wished they had a plan. It is used for a discussion during one of the first formal mentor-mentee meetings For example, having a plan for a simple procedure such as handing

in papers or getting a tissue can prevent unanticipated moments of disruption. When it comes to routines and procedures, being reflective, instead of reflexive, is important. Reflective means there is time to think about it. Reflexive is acting in response to an event. While we cannot predict every event that may happen in a classroom, we can be reflective about the ones we know happen often. This begins with having already thought about and committed to print these important components. In other words, just having an idea in your head isn't enough. It needs to be recorded and hopefully even discussed. Mentors and principals also find the plans helpful during conversations about classroom management. It is a working document that can be a great tool for getting started in the school year, as well as for checking in to find parts of the plan going well and the areas that might need to be considered for further work in developing and implementing. (See Sample Classroom Management Plan #9a Elementary & #9b Secondary in the Appendix.)

> When it comes to routines and procedures, being reflective, instead of reflexive, is important.

Reflection Opportunities

A reflective practitioner is an effective practitioner. We want reflective practitioners and need to cultivate an environment for this to happen as a normal part of the culture. Riding the waves of change in education might be the most underrated skill we focus upon. There are changes that take place daily, in a few months' time, or over the course of a school year. There are the big changes we see over time when we have become practitioners with some time and seasoning behind us.

Learning to surf in the ocean does not happen without practice and neither does riding the waves of change in a classroom, building, or district. Alexandria Spalding (2024) states:

> Schools with a reflective teaching culture have an edge in times of rapid change. The shift to blended and online teaching as a result of Covid-19 in 2020 is a great example.

Even the most experienced teachers found themselves in uncharted waters. Strategies needed to be reconsidered and delivery forms adapted to the new learning environment. Reflection, collaboration and iteration were critical skills and key for adapting quickly in challenging times.

While some beginning teachers may be reflective practitioners from the start, others may need more practice and support in becoming one. When overstimulated, just plain exhausted, or overwhelmed with a day, it is easy to bypass being reflective. No one wants one more thing to think about! This is why we need to build in those opportunities to ensure they happen.

Reflexive responses are an immediate reaction to situations that may or may not have been anticipated. Reflection is looking back upon a situation and evaluating the merits and challenges, as well as whether to continue as planned or make changes. Both are a part of the teaching profession. There are simply some things one cannot anticipate happening no matter how long a person has been working with students. While this is part of the job, it is also important to find ways to reduce the number of reflex moments and plan effectively to do so. While one can't always plan for every situation, knowing the most common ones and being able to recognize them when they occur are important. Constantly having to be in a reflexive mode can be exhausting for any teacher. When a teacher's brain is already making many decisions in mere seconds to minutes at a time, figuring out how to reduce the surprises can make the job much more enjoyable for both the teacher and the students. Providing reflective practice opportunities can help hone that skill. Reflection allows for self-feedback and a critical look at the effectiveness of how all things teaching might be going. What is going well, not going well, and possible options for next steps are self-feedback opportunities.

The more reflective one can become, the fewer reflex responses are needed and the smoother a teacher's day, week, month, or year can become. How do we help build upon the skill of being a reflective practitioner? Here are a few ideas.

2 Two CC's/Glows and Grows/3-2-1 Protocol

Beginning training for any sport or skill requires gaining fluency, repetition, and skill development while also not dreading every second of the process. You want the workouts of basic skills to help increase performance while also making sure they don't diminish joy of the activity. Therefore for new teachers, provide reflection opportunities which are important while also making them doable and not tedious. Anything that takes time away from doing what is necessary needs to be a valuable use of time that contributes to the bigger goal. One way to make this manageable is weekly reflection opportunities via email, vlog, or personal conversation. One example of this that has worked is a weekly email in our district I called the two cc's (a "dose" of celebration and challenges). When medical doctors prescribe medicine, it is in the amount of "cc's." In education, prescribing small reflection opportunities is also good for what will help a teacher get better. And in this case, the cc's stand for a celebration and a challenge. The two cc's are a short email with a few words of encouragement, information, or tips, along with a request for new teachers to share a celebration and a challenge from the week. It is easy to often focus on the challenges as there are usually many. Remembering to also focus on what went well is important, too. By doing this weekly, it is easy to spot any patterns that might be occurring that need additional support or attention, as well as good conversation starters if a mentor, coach, or principal is checking in. One of the advantages of using email to do this, the teacher can choose within a set time period when to respond. The weekly reflection creates a sort of diary of the year. It is enlightening to save the two cc's for a teacher's first year, and at the end of the year create a booklet of beginning teachers' reflections to give to each of them. Here is an example of what an exchange of two cc's might look like.

From the Support Team:

> You have been in school with students for four weeks! Some days may feel like they've been forever and other

days may seem to be flying by. We will continue to problem solve, learn, and adapt along with the students. Be kind to yourself. You may be working both mentally and physically the hardest you've ever worked to keep so many balls in the air. It will get better.

Please schedule a lesson planning conversation with me. I also want to help you with your focus/intention based on our last PD. Keep the questions coming! You really are off to an amazing start.... even if some days don't feel that way!

Tap me your two cc's.

Sample reply from beginning teacher:

My celebration of the week was completing my first IEP meeting. It went really well and I was able to take great notes to help me in the future. My challenge for the week was with my 4th and 8th hours. We have ended the week much better than we have started so I am looking forward to them carrying it over into next week (or so I hope).

Thank you!

New Teacher

Other similar quick-to-implement ideas for reflection opportunities include Glows and Grows or a 3-2-1 protocol. Glows are the positive points and grows are the next steps for learning or elevating to the next level. The use of a 3-2-1 protocol is an example of reflection protocol that can be adapted in many ways for all content areas and most grade levels. There are many that can be found for both teachers and students. Oftentimes, these are examples of formative assessment opportunities as well.

Questioning

Other reflection opportunities can be supported through intentional questions and the role of effective feedback being a common or normalized part of the school culture. Evaluation visits and conversations should not be the only opportunities to talk about student learning and instruction. Finding ways to support thinking and coaching teachers toward their goals can help move them forward. Sometimes this is more effective than consulting with them to give the answers or suggestions for next steps or what to do. This should happen often to help develop the thinking process as a normalized part of what teachers do.

Some examples of questions to ask to help promote teacher reflection:

- What went well? How did you know?
- What did not go as well as planned? How do you know?
- If you were to do this lesson/plan/project again, what would you continue to do the same?
- If you were to do this lesson/plan/project again, what would you change?
- What is something you are proud of today? This week? This quarter?
- What is your next step in learning?
- What keeps you awake at night or are thinking about when you leave for the day?
- What has been your biggest surprise?
- What has gone as you anticipated? How did you know to expect that?

These are just a few of the many possible questions to elicit conversation and thinking. As teachers grow into more experienced reflective practitioners and learners, they can then guide students in doing the same.

Communicate and Then Again

With new information, situations, curriculum, and all of the daily "new" situations or questions that come with the beginning of teaching, it is easy to overlook, forget, or misplace information, emails, paper, and whatever other item that might appear during the day. Keep in mind, communication is different for the person *who* sends it than for the person who receives it. What seems clear to the sender can be murky or confusing to the receiver. Finding systems to provide reminders will help ensure communication is strong. Teachers may have a perceived lack of communication that is often not acknowledged by the sender. Fortunately, digital communication makes it simpler to schedule reminder emails, share calendar events, and provide audio and video explanations. Much like students in a classroom, finding multiple ways to reach learners and having routines in place to provide consistent systems of communication and information retrieval will only help the communication pipeline be strong. New teachers may not always understand what items of information and tasks are priority, what is "good to know," and what are the things to schedule for another day. This is another part of the learning process to assimilate, along with the many other facets of the job. As professionals we expect a certain level of professional responsibility for being organized, remembering deadlines and tasks to complete, and organization to make them happen. These skills have to be developed and refined more for some teachers as a part of growing as a professional, and even the organized people sometimes need reminders.

> Keep in mind, communication is different for the person *who* sends it than for the person who receives it.

Organization

When a large number of emails are coming in, papers are filling the school mailbox, and students are submitting documents either digitally or on paper, keeping track of and finding these things easily will be important. Valuable time can be lost seeking important job embedded components without a system or playing catch-up to forgotten jobs needing completion. Less apparent is the understanding that a well-organized approach to teaching and student learning can also impact classroom management. It is important to recognize that each person may have a different way of organizing or managing large amounts of information and items. Yet, it can also be overwhelming for new teachers when they don't realize the vast array of those things they will need to organize. A few tips for helping them to get started organizing might include:

- Encourage keeping a list of things to remember, either digitally or written, and using a calendar to prioritize when items need to be completed
- Provide storage containers and organizers for getting started (or take advantage of sales at local stores or garage sales)
- Provide frequent reminders
- Help them develop a plan for how students submit work, papers are graded, and grades recorded
- Support them in developing a plan for how to have students become part of the process of keeping the room clean and organized
- Encourage them to set a timer for work segments to focus on a few things to complete during a set period of time
- Explore efficient strategies for grading work, as well as recording grades to include a plan for absent students, as well as a late work system

Conflict Resolution Skills

As new people are assimilating into a grade level, building, or district, team building takes time and can go through different phases of development. While navigating many personalities is as varied as people themselves, the potential for conflict is as likely as the sun rising each day. Team building can take many forms, as well, with colleagues, parents, students, and even community members. Conflict can rarely be avoided and is often necessary for growth and improvement. Being prepared to deal with it in a professional manner can be very helpful and not a skill always taught or addressed until the need arises.

As mentioned before several times, modeling will be one of the most important strategies to help support beginning teachers in learning how to face challenges such as conflict. When they see their colleagues and leaders address conflict in a positive and professional manner, they will be more likely to do so.

Taking a proactive approach can also help provide the tools before they are needed. Addressing the proper steps for handling conflict in advance can be helpful. It is much easier to discuss potential issues and steps for handling them before they occur and when emotions are not involved. Provide suggestions of language to use and even role-play situations to ease tension. For example, share scenarios in which a teacher may need to call a parent regarding a student's behavior or grades as a potential opportunity for conflict to occur. Grade level partners or departments may have to come to consensus on items throughout the year. It is also a part of human nature to experience personality conflicts in the workplace. Having a proactive process in place before conflicts arise could prevent a world of misunderstanding that does not come to the surface early enough to address it.

Roles of Support

Support in the classroom for teacher instruction, student learning, and any potential challenges that may occur is often the role of an instructional coach, mentor, and/or principal depending on the situation of each school. To best meet the needs of individual teachers, this type of specific support takes more planning and thought. For those providing this type of support, guidance and training in understanding how to best provide feedback and growth opportunities from within a classroom are highly recommended. Learn about the roles of the coach, consultant, and collaborator and when each role is most appropriate to elevate the experience of support. Most critical will be distinguishing between those who are providing classroom support, such as the coach, collaborator, or consultant, and where and with whom the role of the evaluator lands. Be clear when keeping the evaluation process out of the equation when providing support. Anytime there is a second person to provide support, dialogue, or as a thought partner, it makes the experience richer, especially if they are not the evaluator as well. This may happen from a new teacher mentor or instructional coach who are important in providing support in many different ways. Retired teachers have also been used as a support system. Planning how the support will be provided with clear guidelines for expectations of both the new teacher and the provider should be explained before beginning.

Initiative Follow-up Support

School districts, buildings, departments, or grade levels may have specific initiatives or curriculums they prioritize. Training for these things can be provided for new hires before school starts or once the year begins. It may be overwhelming juggling a new job or school and all of the new learning that goes with it, along with absorbing additional new training information. Once students are in the classroom and implementation begins, what once seemed clear in training might not look the same in practice. It is important to plan for and schedule follow-up support for teachers (new and old) to make the most effective use of a practice. Short meeting opportunities to discuss current challenges or upcoming lessons, a scheduled time to ask clarifying questions, or watching the implementation in real time can be useful once the teacher has had a little time to put the initial training and information into practice. For example, it is helpful to have a new teacher watch a reading or math lesson (or several) in an experienced teacher's classroom or have someone come in to model a strategy or lesson with their class at the beginning of the year. Follow-up throughout the beginning of the year and during other times can help ensure the fidelity of the work, as well as the confidence of the teacher.

Grading periods can also create an added stressor. Helpful conversations for a new teacher to make them feel prepared are providing opportunities for discussion around grading practices, the timeline and process for submitting grades, the expectation and suggestion for adding comments, and communication with a student's caretakers.

✅ Key Takeaways

- Implementation in the classroom of new learning is needed for results in student learning and professional growth. This can happen in big and small ways yet needs intentional planning to be most effective.
- Communication, classroom management plans, reflection opportunities, organization skills, support systems, and initiative follow-up are some key areas for additional professional development areas beyond instruction.

Section 3
POLISHING THE APPLE

10

Celebrating and Reflecting

The fast-paced world we live in often doesn't provide moments or time to pause, reflect, and appreciate the positive aspects of our lives. We are also often surrounded by more negative messaging than positive messaging. It takes an intentional effort to create experiences that allow people to breathe in success and joy. For some, these experiences are deemed a *waste of time* when more pressing issues await all of us in our inboxes. But allowing individuals to reflect upon, think about, and celebrate their successes is truly food for the soul. It is a proven motivator and gives people permission to feel good about the work they do. The leader must imagine and implement these moments for everyone in the organization but especially our new staff. They can often feel overwhelmed and begin to only focus on what isn't going well. Please take this job of celebrating seriously and begin to envision the ideas presented in this chapter.

Inspiration and Celebration

Teaching is tough, and first-year teachers need motivation to make it through the year. Who are we kidding? Sometimes all teachers need motivation to make it through a year! Simple gestures can go a long way in helping someone to feel appreciated

DOI: 10.4324/9781003487470-15

and as a valued member of a learning community. Small interruptions at just the right time can be the boost to keep morale up.

Here are a few celebration ideas:

1. Create a beginning of the year Getting to Know You form to find out a favorite drink or snack and provide that as a surprise, pick-me-up, or celebration.
2. Write a handwritten note or encouraging and positive email, which can go a long way.
3. How about a new teacher shower? A staff in a building, grade level team, or department can "shower" the new teacher with welcome notes or cards containing snippets of their best advice and tips, or small, but helpful "getting started" gifts such as sticky notes, pens, paper clips, and other useful tools that add up in cost when needing to be purchased all at once.
4. Introduce and highlight your newest talent department members aka new teachers to the staff and/or community via newsletters, social media, emails, or other communication tools regularly used. Share their interests, fun facts, and anything else that might be a way for others to find out more about them and make connections.
5. Video students sharing something they like about their teacher or saying thank you and play it at a meeting.
6. Schedule a group fun-only event for new teachers and mentors to enjoy together.
7. Have an end of the year celebration. Toward the end of the year afterschool, we invite our mentees, mentors, and administrators to celebrate those completing their first year of teaching. There is food, recognition of mentor/mentee pairs, scrolling pictures from throughout the year, and usually some type of activity that brings laughter and reflection on the year. It takes less than an hour and is a positive way to wrap up the year.
8. In a National Association of Secondary School Principals article, Abbye Duggins (2018) recounted an inspiring activity in which her school participated:

We participate in the 25 Wonderfuls project, inspired by Rebecca Leigh's the 50 Wonderfuls Project, which asks supportive friends and mentors of the beginning teachers to share 25 Wonderful things about them. In January, we organize an Induction Teacher Celebration where we play Networking BINGO and listen to TED-style talks from attendees. The celebration concludes with a video of students expressing their appreciation for their first-year teacher, which was filmed secretly with the help of their mentors.

9. When I first started as a coach, each month I had cute motivational tokens such as candy with clever sayings, small gifts of appreciation, and food as pick-me-ups. These were small surprise reminders of staying positive and letting the person know they were being thought about. I later came to realize these were like the rush of a good ice cream cone or the educational high of a motivational speaker. Those can be short bursts of energy that may have a temporary boosting power. What makes those gestures mean more? Personalized recognition, a short note or kind word, recognition among peers, a professional-to-professional thoughtful discussion when trying something new, follow-up in a timely manner to questions, small notices, specific feedback, support during a tough time, providing a break during the day and knowing what someone may need.

✅ Key Takeaway

- ♦ Finding small and big ways to celebrate new teachers is important, too.

11
Support the Supporters

Behind every successful teacher there should be a village that supports their efforts and lifts them up in times of need. Behind every new or beginning teacher, this village needs to have a laser focus on the new teacher's needs to survive and thrive. The new teacher support system needs to include mentors, peers, instructional coaches, principals, and other district personnel. All of these individuals need to understand the individual needs of the new teacher while at the same time having the resources and training to meet these unique needs. Careful consideration must be given when choosing mentors, and suitable training must be provided for them. Mentors should also be provided with useful materials and time with their mentees to make the most of their journey together. Additionally, mentors can help their mentees navigate teacher well-being and assist them in becoming a complete professional. This relationship can become an essential key to the success of a new teacher.

Support for Mentors

> "My mentor always asked me: *Did you do something to change a student's day today, no matter how small?* If I answered yes, then I'd done my part for the day. I still ask myself that question." —*Kelly H.* (Crowley, 2015)

Mentors are often considered one of the front-line supporters of beginning teachers. They might be a person who sees a beginning teacher on the most frequent basis or has the most knowledge of their content area. As the above quote from Kelly H. shows, they can have a long-lasting impact on their mentees. Mentoring programs vary among school districts according to stipend amounts, training, availability, and how they are chosen. Often mentors are also classroom teachers who have their own group of students to teach.

In a conversation, an experienced teacher who enjoyed mentoring beginning teachers said, "I support my mentee after school when we have our weekly meeting and talk about what they need. I love supporting a new teacher. The challenge is that then I have to spend the next hour after school doing my own work." This is certainly worth remembering and considering as you evaluate your own mentoring program. Already established dedicated time and classroom coverage to allow the mentor time to meet with their mentee, observe their mentee, or attend professional development opportunities together should be decided well before it is needed. Any way to help make the additional time commitment valued, albeit it a stipend, additional time, or some other way to say "thank you," when done well it needs to be recognized as a big commitment.

Mentors can be supported by building principals and instructional coaches in many ways. A good start is to provide tools that are easily accessible for requirements or resources. Having any required paperwork readily available in a digital format, providing access to mentoring requirements via videos or digital slides, and a point person for questions are just a few examples. Sometimes just knowing what to say or asking a new teacher to get them talking and find out more can be helpful. A conversation starter can be open-ended questions to ask their mentee at different times of the year based on common new teacher needs and concerns.

Here are some examples of mentor support tools/resources:

- ♦ Line of continuum (see Line of Continuum #10 in the Appendix): This is a helpful tool for mentors and mentees to complete to quickly learn about working styles and tendencies. It is a great prompt for conversations about preferences and how each works best. Complete this at an initial meeting or early in the start of the support process. Learn about and discuss these things in a proactive setting to prevent possible conflict later due to lack of understanding each other's work habits and general preferences.

- Provide general getting-to-know-you information from a survey completed by the new teacher they are supporting. This might include general information such as hometown, family members, other jobs held, favorite snacks, best way to contact, etc.
- Mentoring memos (see Mentoring Memo Examples #11 in the Appendix): These are weekly or monthly emails with reminders, tips, and suggestions for all things mentoring. They should be timely based on having a good understanding of the needs of the mentees as a group and might offer questions to spark conversations.
- Classroom coverage: Provide a substitute teacher to cover the mentor's classroom to allow time to work with mentees or find an opportunity for them to do something enjoyable together.
- Appreciation posts: Remember to say thank you for the value of their work to the beginning teacher.
- Easy access to paperwork/documentation and information needed to complete the mentoring requirements and streamlining any documentation.
- A mentoring toolkit with ideas for welcoming a new teacher, support/language for discussion, example/non-examples of questions, situations and topics to discuss, checklists.
- Share challenges: Educate mentors about the phases of a first-year teacher and other common challenges, along with ways to support the challenges.
- Opportunities for collaboration: Much like new teachers, mentors could find it helpful to have short opportunities

for collaboration with other mentors or attend short PD sessions to learn how to best support their mentee.
- ♦ <u>Opportunities to have fun/relax</u> and enjoy one another. This could be a lunch together, team building event, or intentional positive focuses.

Mentor and mentee relationships are important to help foster. It is an interesting dynamic between colleagues. A mentor is asked to serve as a coach to guide and support, a collaborator to work beside the mentee, and a confidant to be a supportive person to lean on. They should never be in the role of an evaluator. For someone who has never been a mentor, they may only know the value of one based on their own experience, either positive or negative. A planned mentor support system should also be considered. Finding ways to go beyond a beginning of the year one- or two-hour training session for mentors can be helpful in strengthening the program.

Choose mentors thoughtfully, considering those who are willing and capable of providing the best support. Some individuals genuinely enjoy mentoring new teachers and willingly take on the role year after year. It is a commitment of additional time beyond their own classroom and students. Others who accept a mentoring role may feel obligated or compelled to mentor without the same level of enthusiasm. Each school district must develop its own strategies for recruiting mentors and determining appropriate compensation for their work, while also outlining their expectations. *Excellent teaching in the classroom may not always translate to being an effective mentor.* Additionally, it is equally important for beginning teachers to have dedicated time each week to receive support from their mentors. A negative mentoring experience can significantly impact the mindset of a new teacher. For newly hired, experienced teachers, having a "buddy teacher" or someone available to answer questions, especially during the initial stages, is highly valuable.

Mentor accountability is also important. Leaders should consider how they will keep a pulse on the mentor/mentee working together. In most situations, the mentor is receiving a stipend. Avoid waiting until the end of the year to find out a beginning teacher has had limited support from a mentor. Use surveys, conversations, and an accountability process to ensure time is being spent supporting a mentee. Provide a system that is manageable for all parties involved (mentor, mentee, administration).

Support for Educator Well-Being

A supportive and generally satisfying working environment is a goal for all districts and buildings. The work environment has an impact on job performance and affects student learning. When a new teacher knows the options for handling a struggle, who to go to for various questions or concerns that arise, feels supported through mistakes and celebrations, and has the opportunity for collaboration and fun, the days may feel long, but the time can seem short and manageable in a new job or location.

Stress is unavoidable in most any profession, and the education world is no exception. It may take many forms depending on many factors. Strategies for dealing with stress and a proactive focus on teacher well-being may not always be a priority focus or planned learning opportunity. Social-emotional learning (SEL) has gained a lot of attention in schools when considering the needs of students. One might also consider this an important focus for our educators given the statistics of teachers leaving the profession, many of whom have taught less than five years. Kristina Scott, Ed.D. (Scott, n.d.) writes:

> Burnout has three key dimensions associated with it: emotional exhaustion, depersonalization, and reduced personal accomplishment. All of these factors result from chronic emotional and interpersonal stressors in the work environment (Maslach, Jackson, Leiter, Zalaquett, & Wood, 1997). It is interesting that this is exactly what SEL competencies are focused on building resilience in— how to cope with emotional and interpersonal stresses and challenges. Perhaps, before we focus on adding SEL skills for our school-age children, we need to embrace SEL development in our teachers.

Finding ways to provide the important things that help teachers feel supported can come in various forms. While each person has their own version of what is most meaningful to feel supported, there are some generalizations that can be put in place.

Professionalism support: Expectations may have been explained, along with a lot of other information, throughout the start of the school year. This information usually came at the same time as a multitude of other things to remember. Words of support or suggestions and ideas are also usually plentiful when everyone is motivated by the excitement of the new school year ready to launch. Dig a little deeper into the support options during the hub of induction to provide what is needed to better understand and navigate the challenges and unanticipated components of the job. Remember to revisit the 4 c's of culture, compliance, clarification, and collaboration throughout the year.

How can a person know the nuances of a district or school? Every school has its nuances, characteristics, and personalities that make up their culture. What does professionalism look and sound like for themselves, as well as in the culture of the building? This is often a tone set by the building administrators. Knowing what to wear; how to handle challenges from students, parents, and colleagues; the expectation for arrival/departure of students and teachers; and attending meetings, giving assessments, gathering data, and other daily tasks might not be apparent to everyone. It takes a lot of thinking, organization, and intentionality to keep it all straight and together. Meanwhile, lesson planning, managing the classroom of students, and providing learning opportunities for all are vying for time and priority. Balancing each of these is not a necessarily skill taught in a college class or learned elsewhere.

Provide examples to genuinely model what is most important. In other words, walk the walk versus talking the talk. Start with modeling and examples proactively instead of reactively. Be able to use models and examples to explain the importance of certain things prior to any problems occurring; this will reduce the opportunities for the problem to arise. For example, if parent communication is a highly valued part of a school's culture, provide new teachers the opportunity to practice mock phone calls and sit in on other parent phone calls to listen. Have available example emails and provide a list of dates for school sponsored parent events throughout the year. Principals who want a teacher to provide interactive instruction should model examples during meetings. Do you want them to feel comfortable trying new ideas and possibly failing in the process? Will they see their leader do the same and be able to watch this person embrace the failure as a learning opportunity? Even something as simple as providing a resource to share what professionalism looks and sounds like in your building or classroom can be very helpful for a new teacher to use in navigating all the uncertainties of a new job and starting in the profession. Suggestions and tips such as the importance of being on time, answering emails in a timely manner, social media awareness, and suggestions for district professional dress guidelines can be a proactive approach to helping all new hires be informed.

Some schools have professional development focused specifically on self-care and stress management. The goal may be to renew the reminder that learning, and enjoyment of life, can go together. Fun activities such as group games, yoga, food prep classes, and meditation moments to help refuel can be valuable time spent. When planning for support systems, know the needs of the staff and be mindful to not create more stress. Spending time doing fun activities is only as helpful as the to-do list awaiting when the fun is over. Provide a balance or choice. When time is a treasured resource, use it wisely.

> Spending time doing fun activities is only as helpful as the to-do list awaiting when the fun is over.

✅ Key Takeaways

- Mentors, instructional coaches, and anyone else supporting new teachers need resources, training, and a plan for how to best provide support.
- A mentor is asked to serve as a coach to guide and support, a collaborator to work beside the mentee, and a confidant to be a supportive person to lean on. They should never be in the role of an evaluator.
- Other supports may include teacher well-being and learning the ins and outs of being a professional.

12

Love a Teaching Life

Let's be honest. Most of us really do get into this profession because we have a soft spot for our students and truly love the craft of teaching. Teaching a lesson that engages students while helping them master new content is truly an "education high" for a classroom teacher. The joy in teaching fills our souls. Many new teachers begin with this joy and quickly experience numerous challenges that can start to diminish the shine of their chosen profession. It will be important to help new teachers retain their initial joy and continue to find those moments of delight in the classroom. Assist them in finding connections with their peers and the community. Continuously support their journey to achieve work/life balance and keep a watchful eye out to help them navigate elements of the system that seem clear to you but can also be hidden for them as new employees. Keep their spark for teaching alive through the support systems you put in place for them.

> Conversations and connections are important for beginning teachers.

Social Opportunities

Conversations and connections are important for beginning teachers. Social opportunities within and outside the school day can provide a time for much needed decompression from the job with others who can relate to the challenges. Everyone has to eat, so anytime food is involved, it is a great invitation attraction. From an ice cream sundae bar to appetizers after work, any opportunity for teachers to get together to talk about their day, their challenges, and anything else that makes it an enjoyable time together is a greatly valued opportunity. Some areas may have organizations for young professionals or offer specials for teachers. Others may have families willing to invite teachers to their homes for dinner or to play games. Keep in mind that new teachers will have full plates of responsibilities at school and may not always have the time or think they have the time to stop and socialize. It is important to consider this when thinking about social opportunities. Keep the time frames short, allow for easy coming and going, and offer free food to attract more teachers. Social opportunities can also begin before school starts to provide a time for returning and new teachers to gather to meet.

Other ideas:

- gather at a local teacher supply store to share resources
- board or yard game night, bonfire
- coffee chat at local coffee shop
- ice cream sundae bar
- grading and grazing night
- paperwork and pizza

Community support can be another consideration:

- Adopt a new teacher program to pair a community member or business with a new teacher to provide a welcoming environment.
- Connect with a local retired teachers' group to find ways to work together for snacks at meetings, support new hires with a hello, or host a meal.
- Work with the local Chamber of Commerce to coordinate "swag bags" with local business contributions.

- Design a scavenger hunt to visit local businesses to receive coupons or prizes.
- Create a list of "teacher discount" businesses in the community.
- Contact a local young professionals' network or community group to introduce new hires to the community.
- Contact local churches, civic organizations, or community groups to provide snacks, needed supplies, or items along with the opportunity to have their name connected with the gesture.

Work-Life Juggle

A commonly used phrase is "work/life balance." The phrase is promoted to emphasize the importance of ensuring the likelihood of job satisfaction and reducing burnout by striking a balance between personal life and work life without one interfering with the other. This phrase implies that both work and life beyond work should be equal to achieve. Balance seems to imply 50/50, half, or exactly even. I would suggest this is misleading and hard to obtain or even measure. Work/life juggle might be a more realistic term to consider when supporting educators, especially the newest ones. I think it is fair to suggest that in many professional jobs there are times when one requires or allows more time than the other. It might be reasonable to expect they won't necessarily always be in balance, but instead to strive for opportunities where one doesn't stay tilted one way too long so that the other is greatly affected.

> Work/life juggle might be a more realistic term to consider when supporting educators, especially the newest ones.

Have you ever been in a driving situation where you had to turn down the radio in order to focus and to help you "see" better? Our senses tend to work better when we can focus on only a few things at a time when intentional focus is needed. Our brain only has so much capacity when we need to hold onto information and process it at the same time. This is an example of channeled focus, and it has a capacity that can only hold so much at a time. Trying to balance this channeled focus between school and life outside of school can sometimes be hard to shut on and off in either place when starting a new job, beginning in the profession, or when life events are occurring. A few tips and ideas to help new hires keep it all in perspective might include:

- Encourage teachers to set 1–3 days a week that they will stay later to work, but to leave by a certain time on the other days. Have an accountability partner to help them stick to it.
- Use a timer to stay focused on tasks that need to be done to reduce distractions.
- Find ways to show that family and life outside of work is valued by getting to know the teacher's needs, family, and interests.
- Require that emergency substitute plans be made and available in the event of a sub being needed with no time to make plans.
- Limit the number, if any, of committees or meetings a beginning teacher is asked to be a part of their first years.
- Help teachers know what to prioritize and most important when deciding where and how to spend their time. What are the negotiables and non-negotiables?

Hidden Rules

We ask teachers to spend time being very clear with students about expectations for behavior and learning in the classroom. It is equally important that teachers new to a district and building have multiple opportunities and resources for knowing the same for their job. What are the compliances that should be at the forefront of all decisions and along with clarifications that might be assumed instead of stated? When evaluating your hub of induction for strengths and areas to grow, here are some questions for consideration:

- Is there clarity of expectations for job performance, work relations, and for learning for both students and teachers?
- Where are the opportunities for choices and what are the non-negotiables? There are many things in a building or district that are non-negotiable and standard expectations. This might be something specific such as how and when to communicate with parents, homework, building rules, or teaching a certain program.
- What might be implied expectations that we forget to let others in on knowing? These are things such as pet peeves of the principal, how meetings should run, and what (and not) to bother the secretaries about. Sometimes these are referred to as "the hidden rules."

It is sometimes emphasized to classroom teachers the importance during instruction of both teachers and students knowing what they are to learn, how they know they have learned it, and what is the next step if they do not know. Also, throw in the classroom procedures and rules which should be clearly stated, reminded, and reinforced to provide an optimal learning environment. Do we do the same for our teachers upon joining a district and building? How are these shared and able to be referred to if they are forgotten? What are the things for which you want teachers to be sure they know they have autonomy? While it might be implied or mentioned during the interview process and maybe addressed during orientation, having a clear understanding and reminder of this would be important.

✅ Key Takeaway

- Social opportunities, learning to juggle work and life beyond school, and hidden rules are other important points to consider when supporting new teachers (as well as all teachers).

13

Additional Considerations

This chapter focuses on the teachers that don't always fit neatly into your well-designed induction process. You must be flexible and ready to support teachers who are hired during the year. They will need the same intentional guidance you provided your new teachers that started at the beginning of year while also needing assistance catching up with all that has transpired at the school before their arrival. They will also be feeling behind before they get started. Connecting, guiding, and staying in touch with these teachers will be critical to their well-being in their new work environment. This chapter also reminds us about our teachers with specialized expertise that might require slight adjustments to their induction. Special education teachers, art teachers, music teachers, physical education teachers, and the many other non-core content area teachers will be able to participate in much of your induction process. Prioritize the fact that their needs might require some focused attention in their specific area of instruction. Have a plan for these important members of your staff.

Late and Mid-Year Hires

For many reasons, teachers may join the school after the year has started or after official orientation. It can be even more difficult for them to get started. Not only do they have a lot of information to absorb quickly, but they also have a classroom full of students who have already started the school year ahead of them. An articulated plan for these teachers is equally important. The number of teachers who also fall into this category will determine how a district will be providing onboarding/orientation and induction in an expedited way. We want them in their positions as soon as possible. However, ensuring they have the information, tools, and support to be prepared will serve in the best interest of everyone involved.

Determine what is most essential for a new teacher hired later in the process. They truly must hit the ground running. Having an articulated plan in place for what is expected of them from mentoring to meetings will be needed to avoid feeling like they were thrown into deep water to see how well they can swim. Those supporting the new person (mentor, principal, team members, instructional coaches) also need guidance. High intensity support during the transition process will be critical for both the teacher and the students. For example, allow time for the new hire to observe in other classrooms and see how the school day runs prior to starting on their own. Have a person with them as they observe to explain things and be able to ask questions. Other department or grade level teachers who can help with lesson planning, grading, and tasks in the beginning can help the new person transition more easily. The new teacher will need to find ways to build a rapport with the students, while also continuing with content. They will need at least a day or two to focus on community building and getting to know the students and the students getting to know them. A lot of administrative and collegial support will be needed.

> Determine what is most essential for a new teacher hired later in the process.

See the example of a reminder checklist in place for when a few new teachers have started the year at different times. (See Late Hire Checklist #13 in the Appendix.)

Non-Content Area Specific Teachers

Special education teachers, art teachers, music teachers, and the many other non-core content area teachers also need special consideration. While many of the components of a new teacher induction program fit the support needed by all teachers, there are ways in which other teachers may need support in a different way. Special education teachers may need additional support in knowing how to write an Individualized Education Program, modify student work, and the many other rules and regulations that accompany this position. Fine arts teachers and teachers who have content that may be not considered core curriculum may need support more specifically suited to their needs. Helping them to understand their connected role in supporting all curriculum is valuable in creating an atmosphere of learning as a team approach. It is very important to consider their role and plan accordingly to ensure they are also getting what they need to be successful.

Again, throughout the hub of induction, the 4 c's continue to be interwoven throughout the process. A culture of continued support, clear communication of compliance, clarification of expectations, and collaboration with colleagues to bring the best opportunities to students is available from start to finish.

Key Takeaways

- It is necessary to determine what is critical and most essential for the new teacher hired later in the process.
- When planning the right support, provide differentiated support to meet the needs of teachers in areas that may have additional or different expectations or content.

Section 4
IN AND OUT OF THE CLASSROOM

14

The Little Things Are the Big Things

Not everything has to make a big splash to create a ripple effect. Have you ever contemplated words spoken or moments lived hours, days, or maybe even months later? It is possible it was a little thing or small moment in which someone else who spoke the words or created the moment may not have even realized the lasting influence. Even the small things such as a genuine "how are you today?" followed by a dedicated time to find out the answer and interest in a person's life can have a big impact. It might be how words and gestures can make someone feel. Other times, the little things involve having systems in place that prevent frustration or reduce unnecessary stress.

The Power of a Copy Machine

A teacher gets to school early to make it to the copy machine before the buzz of the day starts and beats the crowd that may stand in line awaiting their turn to copy. A teacher running late due to a flat tire rushes at the last minute to make a copy of students' work in class for today. Both discover: the copy machine is not working.

DOI: 10.4324/9781003487470-20

The programs for tonight's band concert are scheduled to be printed once finalized and all spellings for names are checked. Knowing parents may save concert programs with their child's name listed makes it a nice item to have available for the attendees. The ink is running low and smudges show up making the program hard to read. What message does a sloppy program send? When a copy machine in a school isn't working, it doesn't take long to notice. You can usually tell there's a problem by the look on the teachers' faces.

When none of the copiers in a building are working—watch out. It can derail a building and impact the overall atmosphere of the teachers who were depending on using it. What is the power of a copy machine? The copy machine is a piece of equipment that when running fine, no one really notices unless you have to stand in line to wait for it. However, when it stops working, word spreads quickly and frustration builds. The teacher planning to copy today's work has to change plans at the last minute. It might not be that frustration alone to tip the scales of irritation, but it could be one of the several to make a hard day harder. Frustration sets in when something that is usually available and necessary is suddenly no longer an option. It may mean plans have to change at the last minute when the current plans had already taken a long time to prepare, and there is little time or resources to make an alternate plan.

This is an example of a little thing that can make a big difference in the daily work of a teacher. When the little things are added up, they really do become big. It is important to keep a pulse on those "little things" that significantly impact day-to-day operations or key moments within a team, building, or district. A clean classroom, a functional computer, or easy access to resources are just a few others. These may seem like a drop of water in an ocean-like task of getting teachers and staff recruited, hired, and on their way to impacting the learning and education of students for a district. Yet, these seemingly small elements can play a vital role in the smooth functioning of a team, building,

> Seemingly small elements can play a vital role in the smooth functioning of a team, building, or district.

or district. When considering new hires, identifying and prioritizing these little things becomes crucial to planning for success.

Some ideas might include:

- Making sure technology is working
- Providing training and a resource library on any technology support needed
- Showing how to use the copy machine, inner school mail, lunch procedures for students *and* teachers
- Having a library of resources for frequently asked questions
- Explaining rituals of a building—lunchtime, special events, special dress days
- Sharing community good-to-knows—Friday Night Lights sporting events and other large school event gatherings, popular restaurants, doctors, pharmacy, post office, grocery, mechanic
- Providing the dress code, professionalism topics, social media guidelines
- Sharing unwritten rules
- Offering an opportunity to connect with other new hires, social opportunities
- Setting up commuting partners for ride sharing
- Sharing yearly calendar events—take a look at the year events ahead
- Providing access to how district wide announcements are made for things like school closings, important information, etc.

Inevitably, there will be challenges or times when integral systems are not working. The internet goes down, the student information system is not working, or the copy machine is broken are all common challenges that can interrupt a day. Also important is sharing plan B for operation when plan A is not working. Employees will recognize the time, effort, and proactive steps taken to keep the wheels of education in a building or district turning despite the roadside hazards that inevitably occur. In times of challenges or unexpected moments, it is evident and reassuring when a preliminary plan has already been anticipated and considered.

The little things can also be the things a new teacher may never even know about. When their technology is working before they start work on day one or their code is in the copy machine to be able to print off materials for open house night, they won't notice it as being helpful. Yet, it is often these kinds of tasks that take up a lot of time to figure out and can cause undetected frustrations. Where to find the best drink machines and how to use the interschool mail system are the hidden norms or systems easily overlooked once a person has been a part of a building awhile.

What systems or processes in your building or district that when everything is working fine might not be noticed, but when it stops working can cause disruption? What proactive steps need to be taken to prevent those situations? Identifying these things—for both new and returning employees in all the roles of a district—can be important to keeping things running smoothly and efficiently, as well as having a plan in place for when one of those integral systems of operation do take a pause.

More of the Little Things That Really Matter

A getting-to-know-you survey at the beginning of the year can provide information about new hires' birthdays, favorite snacks, or drink. When a mentor, colleague, principal, or other person shows up on a surprise day with a special small treat, the gesture can make a warm welcome feel even more tailored to the person.

At the start of the school year, it is common to have an all-school meeting where various topics may be discussed, including reviewing information from the previous year. When most of the faculty consists of returning teachers, it can be tempting for a school leader to quickly summarize or dismiss certain details by saying, "We go over this every year." As a result, new teachers in the audience may have unanswered questions or require additional clarification but hesitate to ask. It is understandable that meetings need to be concise to respect educators' time. Also recognize that the routine aspects of beginning the year may not be routine and common knowledge for everyone.

To maintain timeliness, sometimes the underlying rationale or purpose behind an action or issue gets cut short. A sometimes-typical scenario is when a group of teachers are collaborating to plan a lesson within a limited 30-minute timeframe. A more experienced teacher may provide a brief overview of the plan and what the teacher should have students do. For instance, they might say, "You will go over these slides with the students and have them complete page 52. Go over the first three together and then let them work on their own." This information is undoubtedly helpful for planning, especially if the necessary materials are readily available. However, essential aspects of the conversation, which could be critically important, are missing. They are the discussion about the lesson's goals, indicators to track student progress (formative checking), common challenges that previous students have faced, key vocabulary, and additional information that could greatly enhance and target student learning. In other words, instead of merely going through the motions of what to do, it is equally vital to explore the significance of the why and how behind the lesson. This is where understanding the curriculum, knowing the priority goals for learning and what the progress of learning looks like is important. Discussion around these topics would be important in helping a new teacher understand student learning and the curriculum.

> Recognize that the routine aspects of beginning the year may not be routine and common knowledge for everyone.

Value their time: "There is never enough time" will always be a huge challenge for all teachers. New teachers in particular feel at the mercy of their colleagues and leaders as the new person on the block. They will be less likely to say no when asked to do something extra and not end a conversation quickly while another obligation is awaiting. A great way to show a new teacher your appreciation for their contributions, is showing them you value their time—by setting time limits on your conversations with them, taking a school day duty for them so they have extra time to work, or offering to help grade papers, run copies, or anything else that might save them time.

<u>Value what they bring to the table</u>: Much of the focus has been on what a school can provide a beginning or new teacher to support their transition and growth. It is also key to recognize the value-added talents and characteristics the new teacher brings to a district, school, and team. Find out their strengths and assets early and highlight those that contribute to the school. Everyone wants to be recognized for what they do well and value being a contributor. When the opportunity to share and be asked about ideas is available, the message is sent that they are a valued member of the community. In addition, being aware of the generalized characteristics of different generations can also be valuable in planning support.

How do you find out what the "little things" might be for your district, school, or team? Ask your most recent newest teachers. Find out what might have been helpful for them when starting out. What caused frustration by not working or having the information needed? Notice what questions seemed to get asked a lot by new hires, both at the beginning and throughout the year. Find out at different points of the year what they remember most and anything that has helped make their job easier. Hold question and answer sessions without a set agenda so that teachers feel free to ask to get the information they need. Consider finding ways for new hires to ask questions in a way that a person hesitant to ask could do so comfortably. All of these avenues for gaining insight and interest in the needs of a new teacher demonstrate that supporting them is a priority.

A new teacher program can be as big or small as needed. Feeling supported as a new teacher is critical. The more support they feel from multiple sources, the more equipped they will be to face the challenges the education profession brings.

The challenge with supporting new teachers can be determining what it looks like, feels like, and sounds like to many different people. A principal, mentor, or instructional coach may feel like they are providing support to a new teacher. However, the person on the receiving end may think differently. Similar to a classroom, each person may have different needs. Finding out what those needs may be takes intentionality. The more intentional the planning and systems that are in place, the more opportunities for feedback and information to provide the most timely and needed support.

Key Takeaways

- Seemingly small elements can play a vital role in the smooth functioning of a team, building, or district and the induction of a new teacher.
- Valuing time and what new teachers bring to the table are additional examples of being intentional about welcoming a new person.

15

It's Not About Being the Best, Just Being Better

Each time a baseball player steps into the batter's box, the result isn't always a homerun. It's great when it happens, but it's unrealistic to expect it every time. In some baseball games, a base hit is worth celebrating and contributes to a team win as much as a big play such as a home run. Every single day of our jobs (and life, too) will not be a home run day. It is important to appreciate the home run moments and reflect upon how to get more of them. Yet, it is not always a realistic expectation for every day. Some days we should be happy with a base hit and celebrate that we didn't strike out. Even in baseball, there are days when the best players strike out at the plate. It is what must happen to help each of us grow and improve. No matter what stage of the game we are at in the education field, we face the challenges and strikeout moments that are a part of playing in the game. Creating a culture and community that can celebrate the little wins and support the moments of strikeouts and hard losses is important. And not just for beginning teachers, but for all teachers. How we react to challenges and react to others is what can make or break the game.

What is the message you want to send to your newest hires when things are not going so great? It is easy to celebrate and high five on the homerun and even base hit days. How about those strikeout days? What do you want them to know about their ability to move forward? A common phrase when talking about classroom management and maintaining expectations is, "It's not what you say, it's what you allow." This is also true when considering the culture of a group if you want progress, innovation, and growth to happen.

> What is the message you want to send to your newest hires when things are not going so great?

While each beginning teacher, just like students, is unique in their own way, there are still challenges that are quite common to all new teachers starting out. It will be important to plan for these common challenges while also discovering those unique to your district, school, or team. Experience has indicated common challenges may include:

- overall classroom operations and regulation
- specific student behavior concerns
- planning and implementation of instruction
- monitoring student learning and connections
- parent communication
- managing time and emotions to navigate all of the above new learning, while also learning how to be a colleague with new coworkers.

Any one of these can be a challenge to navigate in isolation. All of them together can create an ever-evolving feeling of an avalanche of challenges to dodge and address. Those challenges may seem to continue to grow also while new ones pop up. Although there may not be a magic wand to solve the specific challenges for all new teachers, starting with being aware of these challenges and knowing support will be needed is important. Being as proactive as possible is a good start. Also, it's important to have support systems and a timely plan for intervention when challenges do occur. We cannot remove the opportunities of challenges, because that is how a new teacher will grow and learn. We should support them through the challenges and learning, and help to minimize the challenge's level of urgency. This is where the regular meetings with a mentor, instructional coach, administrator, or another support person can be critical. Classroom visits, self-video opportunities, and other professional learning opportunities can provide the help needed.

When you have been in education for a while, it might be easy to wonder why some beginning teachers may not be more transparent about their concerns, ask more questions, or ask for help. Some reasons they may not be forthcoming with concerns is that they may:

> It's important to have support systems and a timely plan for intervention when challenges do occur.

- be unsure what to even ask due to being overwhelmed or lacking confidence in their abilities
- be embarrassed by not knowing answers or feeling as if they should already know the answer
- not want to seem unprepared
- be worried they are being incapable or ineffective and someone will find out
- not want to be a burden to others and disrupt a fellow teacher, mentor, or administrator's busy schedule.

Consider how you might address these concerns in advance before they occur. You can help "the village" of supporters to understand the common concerns, challenges, and plans for support. One of the simplest ways to lend support and learn more about where a beginning teacher might be in their thinking is through conversations and questions. Some possible questions to spark conversations and increase opportunities for helping to gauge successes and challenges are:

- What has been your biggest surprise (today, this week, since starting)?
- What seems to take up most of your time (during class, after school, weekends)?
- What is most stressful for you right now? What keeps you awake at night?
- What small celebrations are you seeing daily?

- What procedures and routines are you still needing to work on with students?
- What is the easiest and hardest part of lesson planning?
- What time of day is best and hardest for your class(es)? Why might that be?
- What do you look forward to learning more about?
- What have you seen or heard another teacher do that you tried or would like to try?
- How have your thoughts about teaching changed?
- If you could change only one thing about your classroom or day, what would it be?
- What do you look forward to each day?
- Six months or a year from now, what do you want to be able to look back and say about this time?

In an anonymous survey of beginning teachers, these are common themes regarding what new teachers wished they told their building principals and administrators.

1. What was most helpful from your principal?
   a. Feedback after an evaluation: both the good and the things needing improvement; be specific; please don't make me wait for days for a follow-up. I'm nervous waiting.
   b. Communication: meeting with you and seeing you regularly matters; an awareness of what is coming up next is helpful compared to being surprised last minute.
   c. Open door policy: It's okay to ask for help; we are terrified to do so.
   d. Your reassurance and help with parents is needed.
2. What I would want a principal to reconsider doing differently:
   a. So many meetings: I need time to figure things out and think.
   b. Talk to me more. Build a connection. Please understand when I ask a question that you sent in an email or may have mentioned in an all-staff meeting, I may have forgotten or not understood.
   c. Ask me what I need instead of micromanaging.

d. Telling me I'm awesome doesn't help me grow, and I don't feel awesome and know I'm not. Tell me what I am doing well and help me get better at the things I'm not.
3. Principals should know this about new teachers:
   a. We are terrified and overwhelmed.
   b. Help us with parents.
   c. We have good ideas, too.
   d. It's hard to talk to your boss about concerns.

Mentors play a huge role in support. This may be a formal position assigned or it may be a role that a fellow educator assumes without a formal designation. Here are some thoughts from beginning teachers.

I would like for my mentors to know:

- I need you to tell me everything about the ins and outs of our school. Help me to think ahead in planning and what is to come.
- Check on new teachers on a regular basis and always be willing to listen.
- I appreciated all that my mentors did for me. I know sometimes I asked some of the most ridiculous questions and probably said some really stupid things, but they truly helped me feel better about things I was doing and going through.
- I appreciate all the time they poured into me during my first year of teaching. Helping me when I didn't even ask for it or volunteering to help make copies means a lot as a first-year teacher. Your willingness to help at any time was appreciated!
- My mentor was an amazing guide who helped me through many challenges. Having another teacher there to talk to when I was dealing with challenges helped me cope with the stress and pressure that you feel in your first year of teaching.
- Feeling supported by another colleague made the world of difference.

- Mentors need to be more available in approaching the new teacher to offer assistance. Many mentors always think the new teacher will come to them, but it can be tough as a new teacher to seek out help and admitting you don't know something.
- Just to be available and sharing lessons is a great help. Planning advice is needed as organization can be a *learned* process. Managing grading papers and putting in grades for students is hard and I need their guidance.
- Lesson planning and discussing student success with my mentor was a great help. It allowed me to make sure I was teaching the curriculum correctly.
- I thank them for all the time and energy they've used in helping me. I love how they are preemptive—thinking of things I would not have and saving me from falling on my face!
- Without my mentor, I would not have the resources to teach to my fullest potential so I am very grateful for having someone I can pull resources from and "steal" any ideas throughout the year.
- That any and all information is important, even the little things. After you've been teaching for a while, I'm sure it's easy to forget the little tasks or routines that you get used to. But these little things or bits of advice are just as important as the big stuff.

These are common themes that have emerged from beginning teachers for their experienced fellow colleagues that might provide insight into planning.

I would like my fellow experienced colleagues to know:

- You intimidate me! I want you to like me and welcome my new opinions.
- I enjoy working as a collaborative team.
- I value their input and knowledge, support, and concern.
- Please share all resources! As a first-year teacher, you don't have any, so any extra copies of worksheets or ideas for games or activities is so helpful. Explain to me the

purpose, ideas, and challenges of the learning to go with it.
- I am new, so no matter how capable I may seem, sometimes I will have to ask questions and possibly several times. Also not to assume too much. I am overwhelmed even though I may look calm.
- I appreciate reminders. I tend to forget things and I have a lot of kiddos, so no, I won't be offended, please ask!
- Teamwork is the only way to manage the workload, and dividing and conquering various jobs can make things more manageable for everyone.
- A kind word from you means the most of all. Know that new teachers feel overwhelmed. Not only have we never done this before, but we don't know anyone. You reaching out to us is a way to pull us into the culture of the school.
- I appreciate encouragement and that just a little, "good job this week" or you "handled that situation really well" would really boost my confidence.
- Their examples provide me with a platform to build my classroom. Their experience is constantly providing me with answers about behavior management, classroom structure, and curriculum development.

<u>Formative feedback for leaders</u>: We ask teachers to provide formative assessments to students as feedback to guide the next learning steps. If we want our new teachers to be reflective, we need to be sure to model this practice with them as well. As a program is being shaped, adapted, or tuned up, the best insight can come from within. The newest teachers can provide information helpful for next steps in support. This is also best practice in figuring out direction and changes to new teacher support. As mentioned previously, tap into the thoughts of current and recent new hires, and do this throughout the year to gain the timeliest feedback. Whether a formal survey can provide the most honest feedback, or a personal conversation will give insight, finding out what is working well and what might need to be improved is important.

This process is equally important for those who are orchestrating the planning, preparing, and implementing the support for new hires. A willingness to be flexible, seek feedback, and recognize when change is needed (and not needed) is critical. Sometimes the "this is how we have always done it" roadblock can challenge the path to keeping up with current needs. Discover the challenges current teachers and the newest hires are facing. Is there any support system that could reduce the level of challenge or resources to aid in the navigation? How are we as leaders learning and growing to improve? Peter DeWitt in a podcast with Jim Knight (Knight & DeWitt, 2023), asked a question that summarized the goal: "How do I help you and get better, too?" Leading by example is the best way to ensure that a growth mindset is part of the culture of improvement. The goal is not to make everyone happy, it is to have a strong foundation in place to build upon. Share the ways you are learning more, getting feedback, and considering new or improved practices to support your newest hires and beginning teachers.

Consider, have I/we:

- provided a way for our newest teachers to provide feedback about the induction, orientation, and onboarding process?
- provided a way for mentors to give feedback about the mentoring support and resources?
- asked the best teachers their thoughts about support for new teachers?
- shared with colleagues or staff resources, articles, or ideas that connect to school culture?
- crafted intentional questions and reflection opportunities for yourself, as well as those you lead/support?
- asked or read what other teams, schools, or districts (or a successful company) do to support new hires?

✅ Key Takeaways

- What is the message you want to send to your newest hires when things are not going so great? Have support systems and a timely plan for intervention when challenges do occur.
- Help "the village" of supporters understand the common concerns, challenges, and plans for support.
- Ask your newest teachers to provide feedback for the support they received.

16

Elevate What You Want to Grow

While not many people love a meeting just to have one, gathering to connect with a leader or learn more to help you do your job better is important. Feeling seen and heard as a part of a team is valuable. The meetings don't have to be long and should be valuable for support and learning. Meeting just to meet when an email could do the same is usually not good use of time.

Assuming every new teacher wants to learn and do their best means modeling excellence in action in your district, building, or team. An important consideration of the support team for new hires is highlighting the expertise and knowledge of the others already doing the work with excellence. Each member of a district, building, or team has a strength. Highlight the strengths of the teachers doing excellent work and allow them to become a resource for the new hires. Consider asking these teachers to be a part of new teacher meetings at the beginning of school or throughout the school year. They can lead or share in a meeting about their strength. Start building the network of support as professionals to expand beyond the team or colleagues the new teacher will be interacting with most often. For example, a new second grade teacher may benefit from learning from a kindergarten teacher who is

> Highlight the strengths of the teachers doing excellent work and allow them to become a resource for the new hires.

good at using the positive language of the school behavior support program. A math teacher might be strong in the beginning of the class routines that would be helpful to all the new teachers in the building. There is usually a teacher who is a technology guru in figuring out the newest building or district technology system. There are many people who are valuable resources within a learning community. Bringing in other teachers from the building to share their experiences and expertise is also a way to build capacity and leadership among staff. One principal who valued teacher leadership held monthly new teacher meetings. Each meeting, the principal brought in a few staff members to share their strength as an educator and provide stories, suggestions, and support for the new hires. Not only did the new hires get a chance to interact with a staff member who may or may not be someone they saw often, but this person shared in leadership and became an ongoing resource "go-to" person for the building. If you want your newest teachers to become like your best teachers, use them to show, tell, and support their learning and growth. What strengths might different people be highlighted and share with new hires?

Another outstanding example of an administrator-led support system is facilitated by a principal who holds a weekly meeting time each week for all building new hires. Once a week for about 15 minutes, she and her new teachers discuss any questions or concerns they have. In addition, she shares a short educational tip or article with them to discuss. It is a quick check-in, time for a short burst of learning, and a weekly opportunity for the new hires to feel supported and touch base with a busy principal. Other principals hold new teacher meetings on a schedule that works for the group with timely topics such as classroom management challenges, parent teacher conferences, grading and report cards, or short book studies. These meetings or learning opportunities can be facilitated and led by the building principal, building teacher leader, instructional coach, or mentor. Most important is that those attending walk away having found the time useful.

Knowing what and who your resources are and utilizing them to help grow and model the work needed to support students will help the planning of opportunities and build capacity for more people to be a support system. Choosing a few key components to implement or focus on growing will likely serve everyone better than doing too many things at once. Also, always going back to the core values and purpose in everything you do will strengthen the results. Remember, you have to be what you want to see. If you want to see teachers being reflective, willing to try new ideas, being vulnerable in asking for help, feeling supported and valued, and willing to ask questions, those characteristics also have to be modeled for them by those who have come before them.

> Choosing a few key components to implement or focus on growing will likely serve everyone better than doing too many things at once.

Key Takeaways

- Administrator-led support systems with planning and intentional implementation can significantly elevate the learning and growth of your newest teachers.
- Highlight the strengths of the teachers doing excellent work and allow them to become a resource for the new hires.

Conclusion
Stoplights

You are driving a long way to get to a destination, and the open road of travel takes you through a town. In this town there are many stoplights that seem to disrupt your progress along the smooth-flowing highway. Now imagine that each time you feel like you have resumed your normal speed and are headed toward your destination, another series of stoplights appear, slowing things down. It wouldn't take long to become frustrated and consider another route. Reducing the unnecessary stoplights, roadblocks, and potholes of the journey for new teachers is key.

Quality induction takes intentional planning. Infusing the pillars of culture, compliance, clarification, and connection in every step requires taking a hard look at what to change and what to keep. The needs at the beginning, middle, and end of the school year are different. Knowing what the needs are and having support in place for each phase of the school year is reassuring to a new hire. The idea that you planned for them, anticipated their needs, and have worked to be a support system for the entire duration of the year and beyond shows a commitment to the educators, as well as students. This intentional practice provides the new teachers with assurance and access to resources which can impact their decision to return the following year.

It is imperative to embrace the fact that once you hire a teacher, the support they need to grow and flourish in your learning community has just begun. It should begin the minute they sign a contract and extend throughout their beginning years in your buildings and districts. It is our hope that you can utilize the ideas in this book to elevate your induction. When you have a process that suits your district or building in place, successful retention of your teachers will grow exponentially. The professional support and development of these teachers is critical to the success of our schools and most importantly, our students. Enjoy your journey with induction. It is a chance to celebrate your learning community and intentionally develop the excellent teachers you have hired. Let's reduce their stoplights and provide them with a clear path to professional fulfillment.

Appendix

Thinking Guide #1

Utilize this planning guide to record existing practices within your school or district. Incorporate new ideas and insights as you engage with the readings and generate further ideas.

Relivables: Our traditions/ things we do that create memorable moments	**Repeatables**: Common questions/ challenges/events
Ideas for consideration:	A place for these to live:

The Village #2

Use this planning guide to inventory the various members of your village within your district or school and their respective support roles for new teachers. Update and expand this list with new insights and information as you gain further knowledge from the book and collaborative team discussions.

Positions/roles	Main support role(s)

Sample Welcome Letter #3

Subject: Welcome to the [Insert District Mascot (ex. Spartan)] Family!

Dear [Teacher's Name],

I am thrilled to extend a welcome to you as the newest member of our [insert district mascot] family! On behalf of the entire school district, it is my pleasure to officially congratulate you on signing your contract and joining us in the great profession of teaching where we can make a difference every day.

You are now part of a community deeply committed to fostering excellence in all our students, as well as employees. At [School District Name], our mission is clear: [insert mission]. Your dedication to this mission is invaluable, and we believe that your passion for teaching will contribute significantly to the success and growth of our students. Together, we will create an environment that ensures that every student reaches their full potential.

Thank you for joining our team. As a community of educators, we know that your unique skills and talents will enhance our school community. We look forward to the positive impact you will undoubtedly make on the lives of our students and the broader school community. Should you have any questions or need assistance as you settle in, please do not hesitate to reach out.

Here's to a successful year ahead!

Sincerely,

[Superintendent's Full Name]

[School District Name] Superintendent

Things to Do Before Orientation #4

This list of ideas can be shared with new hires to provide ideas for those who are eager to get a head start on planning for their school year.

Adapted from Moberly School District S.H.I.N.E. Program

Things you can do before New Teacher Orientation in August (to make life easier for you)

The start of the school year in August can be busy with new information, meetings, and experiences. Here are some tips for things teachers can do before starting their new job and attending orientation in August to help ease the flow of information coming their way.

- Provide your building principal with a current email address and phone number to contact you over the summer.
- Inquire about any summer training you might need to attend.
- Become familiar with the district and your school's website. Look at the activities held throughout the year, school calendar, building faculty websites, and any other information to help you better understand the interactions with your building and district.
- Contact your grade level or subject level team members and introduce yourself.
- Learn about any programs or initiatives that are district or building wide.
- View the online school handbook to become familiar with school policies.
- Familiarize yourself with the standardized testing that takes place in your building.
- Inquire with the human resource department about any paperwork or meeting you may need to attend regarding insurance, certification, etc.
- Compete the classroom management plan.

- If elementary level, become familiar with the literacy and math resources and curriculum materials. If secondary, obtain a copy of any textbooks that will be used.
- Confirm with the principal when you can begin setting up your room.
- Obtain a copy of your class schedule or look at this current year to get a general idea of how it is set up.
- Become familiar with any technology you might be using in your classroom.
- Look at the upcoming school calendar.

Model Classroom Guide Example #5

The model classroom is an opportunity for new hires to get a glimpse into the start of school when students arrive. Creating a general overview of the key components to be modeled and focused upon can ensure consistency if there are several model classrooms taking place. It is equally important to include those elements that are unique to each school, grade level, or content area. The team should discuss and plan for these and tailor them to the most important information.

Model Classroom Overview- Adapted from Moberly School District

Goal of Model Classroom
The goal is to give new teachers essential information specific to their building to start the year smoothly. We also want to cover key components for all classrooms at the beginning of the year, regardless of the grade level or content area.

Please Remember To:
- Make it interactive and engaging with time for discussion and questions
- Focus on what is most important
- Bring the "experienced" but new to the district teachers into the conversation to share their ideas

Example Model Classroom Topics

- What students do when they arrive to school
- Starting class routines
- Explicitly discuss and model key procedures
- What really matters the first few days to get right
- Resources available
- Dismissal procedures
- Special Education information that is necessary
- Community building and why it is important
- Parent communication for the class website, newsletter, etc. expectation for building
- Whom to ask for assistance
- Technology used
- Chromebook expectations
- Common pitfalls of the first few days
- Building relationships, what that really means and looks like

New Teacher Questions #6

New teachers often do not know what questions to ask when getting started. These are sample questions they can have on hand as a resource and guide for "what to ask when you don't know what to ask."

New Teacher Questions to Ask

- Are there any procedures in my Classroom Management Plan that in your opinion I might want to reconsider or should consider adding?
- When is the best time to ask you questions?
- What do I need to know regarding any activities before the first school day (ex. Open House)?
- Where do I find…
  - Textbooks/teacher's manual, what is most/least helpful/important, is there a digital version?
  - My mailbox, inner school mail, copy machine, supplies, teacher restrooms, student records, telephone to make parent calls
  - Nurse, counselor, custodian, any common meeting locations
  - Shared digital files
  - Class list and supplies for students
  - Cleaning supplies, paper towels
- How do I….
  - Make copies, send inner school mail
  - Find my curriculum
  - Use the phone, interactive board, intercom
  - Communicate with parents/families, is there a preferred way or expectation?
  - Deal with an arguing or attention seeking student
  - Do an office referral, when should I do one?

- Where do I…
    - Park upon arrival, be sure not park
    - Check for important information from the principals, secretaries, department heads/grade level chairs, Special Education teachers, etc.
    - Learn more about any programs we might use
    - Eat lunch
    - Greet students in the morning (in room, hallway, gym, etc.)
    - Dismiss students in the afternoon/duties afterschool
    - Take students for lunch/any specials/Explo classes
- What do you notice…..
    - In the classroom as the most challenging transitions for students and how do you address them
    - Being most important for the first few days of school
- What do I need to know about…
    - Students in my classroom with special needs
    - Students with medical concerns
    - Emergency procedures
    - Assemblies
    - Assessments
        - For my grade level/content
        - District wide
    - Using technology/not

- Do you….
    - Have any favorite tech tools or websites/resources you use or would recommend
    - Recommend eating school lunch
    - Have a favorite teaching memory/moment from last year
    - Have a favorite school tradition

Observation Goal Sheet #7

Observation Insights: A Guide
(*Adapted from Moberly School District*)

Use this guide and take notes during your observation. Focus on the points below when reflecting on your own classroom instruction. This is NOT an evaluation of the teacher being observed. Consider what you can learn from their teaching to improve your own classroom practices.

The classroom/teacher I observed: _____

My primary focus of the observation was for me to learn more about:

I chose this focus because:

These are the things I noticed that I will consider for my classroom and student learning:

Post observation reflection stem ideas:

- One thing I noticed that made me think about my classroom was ___
- When observing, I noticed students were_____
- I noticed the teacher……..
  - responded to students by_____
  - positioned her/himself _____
  - started/ended class by _____
  - Used language/phrases such as _____ in order to_____
- I am curious/would like to know more about/was wondering_____
- I found out/learned/am more aware of _____
- Something I would like to consider for my classroom/students/myself_____
- Watching ___ helped me to better understand/know _____
- I saw how to_____
- During the lesson/teaching/learning the students/teacher_____
- I'm not sure about _____

Parent Teacher/Guardian Conference Scenarios #8

Below are six common scenarios for parent/guardian-teacher conference discussions. These can be used to do a role-play and conduct mock conferences. Have a beginning teacher paired with their mentor or experienced teacher to do one-to-one mock conferences. Or the topics may be discussed as a group. Provide example words and phrases for the teacher to use when discussing the student. In addition, discuss common parent replies that may be unexpected.

1. **Student is excelling in class.**
2. **Student is not turning in homework consistently.**
3. **Student is struggling with work/concepts/material.**
4. **Student behavior is a concern.**
5. **Student is struggling to get along with peers.**
6. **Student's poor attendance is impacting learning.**

Examples of scripts to help a teacher. Add to the list and scenarios.

- _____ is a hard worker and demonstrates an attention to (giving thoughtful answers, applying learning to other situations, being very neat, asking good questions).
- I would like to continue to help your child grow by _____.
- What do you notice regarding homework at home?
- When I see _____ (answering many questions in class, doing quality work in class, asking great questions), it lets me know that he/she is learning and understands.
- Has had difficulty with learning _____, so in the coming weeks we are going to focus on_____.
- The thing that I see is holding _____ back from being most successful is _____.
- We are working hard to help _____be successful and grow as a learner to be ready for the next grade. I

notice he/she has missed _____ days this quarter. How can we help get _____ to school/make up what was missed?

Examples of possible parent responses:
What else can we do at home to help?
My child is an A student and making an A-. Why?
My child never brings anything home.
We have a really busy schedule in the evenings.
He/she watches his/her brothers and sisters when they get home from school.
I can't help him/her with the work. I don't understand it myself.
(Might be thinking, but not verbalize…you are the teacher not me. I never did homework or had anyone to help me. Why should it stop my day/evening when I've worked all day and have four kids to feed supper and get to bed. I'm tired.)
Why am I just now hearing about this?
I know, I've tried to talk to him/her, but it doesn't do any good. I don't know what else to do.
He/she said you don't like him/her.
He/she says the other kids pick on him/her.
He/she really hates coming. It is a struggle to get him/her here.
I can't help it when he/she is at his/her __*dad's/mom's*_____ house.

Sample Classroom Management Plan #9a Elementary

(Adapted from Moberly School District)
　　　_____'s Classroom Procedures & Routines
　　　Room #_____

Entering the Room
- Placement of coats/backpack:
- Lunch choices:
- Sharpening pencils:
- Going to breakfast:
- Asking the teacher a question/sharing important info:
- Using the restroom upon arrival:
- Morning work:
- Turning in folders/homework/parent communication:

Leaving the room as a class for recess, specials, lunch, or other events:

- Students are dismissed by:

End of the day dismissal:
- Students prepare to go home by:
- Students are dismissed by:
- How students get home is posted:
- Special considerations and end of the day duties:

Other procedures: For each procedure, it must be clear what the expectation is, what does it look and sound like?

- Using the restroom:
  - During class:
  - As a whole group (lining up, etc.):
- Classroom helpers:
- Sharpening pencils/getting new pencil:
- Using the trash can:
- Getting a tissue:

- Going to the nurse, office, another teacher's room:
- Getting a drink:
- Getting absent work:
- Turning in late work:
- Getting supplies out:
- Organizing supplies in the desk or cubbies:
- Using the computers:
- Asking the teacher for help or attention:
- Moving to carpet from desk/vice versa:
- Sitting on the carpet:
- Recess expectations and procedures:
- Passing out papers:
- Labeling work (name, date, etc.):
- Using a privacy folder during independent work or tests:
- Using the class library:
- When another adult enters the room:
- Transitions during small groups
  - Teacher signal:
  - What does it look and sound like as students transition?

Attention signal(s):

The daily classroom schedule can be found (it should be posted for students, too):

Other things to consider having available:

Early out schedule

Dates for events that might alter schedules

Sample Classroom Management Plan #9b Secondary

(Adapted from Moberly School District)
_____'s Classroom Procedures & Routines
Room #_____

Entering the room
- Bell work/do now:
- Asking the teacher a question/sharing important info:
- Turning in homework:
- Noise level:

Leaving the room at the end of class:
Students are dismissed by:

Other procedures:
For each procedure, it must be clear what the expectation is, what does it look and sound like?

- Using the restroom
  - Before class:
  - During class:
- Answering questions/sharing info during class:
- Tardies:
- Sharpening pencils/getting new pencil:
- Using the trash can:
- Getting a tissue:
- Going to the nurse, office, another teacher's room:
- Getting a drink:
- Going to lockers:
- Getting absent work:
- Turning in late work:
- Getting room supplies:
- Using the lab computers:
- Asking the teacher for help or attention:
- Passing out papers:
- Labeling work (name, date, etc.):

- Handing back graded work:
- Turning in assignments:
- Working independently:
- Taking a test:
- Using the class library/resources:
- Getting in pairs/groups to work:
- When another adult enters the room:
- Fire/tornado/earthquake/intruder drills:
- Proceeding to assemblies/special events:
- Using Chromebooks:
- Going to the counselor:
- Going to the locker room:
- Chromebook issue:

The daily classroom schedule can be found (the students need to see it, too):

Other things to consider having available:

Early out schedule

Dates for events that might alter schedules

Line of Continuum #10

A continuum activity is a way for people to understand each other's perspectives, work habits, personal tendencies, and anything else that might be helpful to know when working together. It is a proactive way for participants to see where along the spectrum others stand on different topics. This is information that can be very helpful to know before beginning to work together.

This can be done in person or using a page. Participants position themselves or mark themselves on a continuum line based on where they align between two statements. Then they discuss why they put themselves in the position along the line.

Possible topics for which the extremes are stated that may be used might include:

- Time of day you do your best work: Early morning (at one end of the continuum)/late night (at the opposite end)
- Your desk is most likely to be: neatly organized/disorganized and chaotic
- Importance of time: will be early/often late
- Planning style: careful planning ahead/in the moment
- Working style: attention to detail/big picture
- Preferred group size: alone/world

Below is an example of what it might look like in paper form.

Continuum Connector

Place a mark on the line to indicate where you see yourself along the continuum for each pair of words.

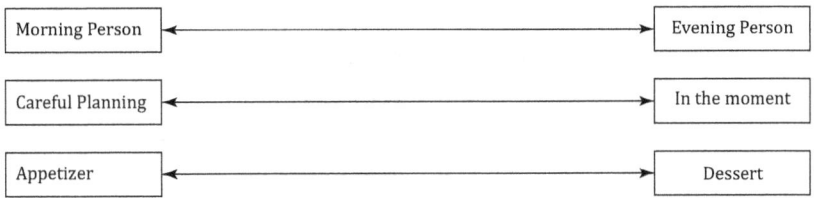

Mentoring Memo Examples #11

Mentoring memos are used to provide mentors with a support connection, reminders, and timely information or resources to help them support their mentees. Here are some examples:

Week #1

Today is an important day. Not only are kids back (yay!), but our beginning teachers have launched day 1 of their career. A few things that seem to happen each year with beginning teachers:

- Today probably went well as the students were nervous, quiet, etc. The beginning teacher thinks it will be this way from here on out, so whatever they told their students today will be remembered.
- They haven't planned for the little disruptions that could quickly become bigger ones, ex: students talking, not following directions, attention seeking behaviors.
- Lesson plans were either finished quickly or went too long.
- Breaking things down into smaller steps or making assumptions about students "getting it" isn't seen as necessary.

Please take time today (and the next few) to reflect with them.

- What went well?
- What was a surprise?
- What did you notice as the day went along?
- What did you notice during bell work, class dismissal, entering class, and teacher talk time?

Go back over procedures as we talked about in training and maybe even add one or two. If we can help them get some things established now, it will pay off for all of us in the long run. We have a great crew. Learning is hard, rewarding, and should be fun, too. Thank you for being a mentor. Your job is very, very important.

Hello Mentors,

Our new teachers are off to a great start! Some of them had the opportunity to student teach, while others didn't have that experience. So we have to help them anticipate those things they may not see coming or know to prepare for. First-year teachers commonly have the following concerns:

- How should I handle students who talk at inappropriate times?
- The classroom procedures went well for the first two days, but today they didn't go as smoothly. What should I do?
- I thought I had a good grasp of lesson planning, but things aren't going as expected. I'm not sure if the students understand, we're moving through the lessons too quickly, and they seem bored or disengaged.

These situations can be frustrating for our new teachers because they start questioning what they thought they knew, and they're unsure about how to address these challenges. Just like their students, our teachers need explicit modeling and information sharing. Here are a few ideas:

- Review their lesson plans and let them explain what they intend to do.
- Ask guiding questions to help them think through the issues.
- Present them with different scenarios to provoke their thinking.

It's important to have two-way conversations where they have ample opportunity to speak and share their thoughts. This will help you understand their thinking processes and provide appropriate guidance. This would be a good time for them to sit in with you as you model a positive phone call home.

Celebrate their achievements as well! This is an exciting time for them as they realize their dreams of becoming teachers, and you are a valuable part of their journey!

Hello Mentors....

Happy Friday! It is so great to read the new teachers' reflections sharing how supported they feel. They recognize things are starting to get tough for them, so THANK YOU for meeting with them weekly and providing support. Our beginning teachers are starting to recognize they don't know what they don't know (disillusionment stage) and situations are arising for which they had not anticipated.

Sometimes they just need to know someone is there....and don't need all the answers. With midterms looming, behaviors of challenging students, meetings, grading, and balancing (or lack thereof) life of school and home, this tends to be the first "season" of great stress. Remember, they will likely tell you "everything is fine" even if it isn't. They don't want to be a bother.

Topics to discuss:

- Sub plans
- Midterms
- Contact parents
- Dealing with specific students and having a plan
- Prioritizing work (reducing grading time, what needs done today, tomorrow, by end of week)?

Remember to have some fun, a few laughs, or even a moment to just get away. We have to keep it real and know that we *all* need some away time and keep things in perspective.

Sample New Hire Plan #12

Plan for Teachers Hired After Orientation

Depending on the size and situation, some districts may have a plan in place for smaller group orientations after the school year starts. Other districts may only plan one orientation at the beginning of the year. This is a general guide to help provide a plan for those districts who only do one orientation.

Starting quarter	Use the late start checklist to be sure critical items are addressed. Give this time to help the new teacher acclimate to all of the new things.
The following quarters to the end of the school year	Begin quarterly requirements (adapt as needed based on the situation and timing).
Start and return to new school year	Participate in new teacher orientation (might only be specific parts of it depending on the needs) at the beginning of the school year. Join the new teacher cohort with the incoming group. This will be on an individual basis determined by the late start date and teacher professional development needs.

Key Reminders to Consider

- The link or directions to access the resources or repeatable tools.
- Information regarding mentor expectations for how often to meet with the mentee and adaptations made for mentor expectations.
- How mentor stipends will be calculated.
- Any professional development expectations for both the new teacher and mentors. Have a clear plan and communication for the meetings that should be attended or not attended.
- Every situation may be unique but having a general plan in place is important.

Examples of a halfway through the school year start. These are the key components and adjustments that should be made according to new teacher needs and district plan.

1st Quarter of teaching = 3rd Quarter of school year:

- Complete the late start checklist (all stakeholders)
- Meet weekly with mentor (mentor/mentee responsibility)
- Begin weekly reflection opportunity
- Work with the instructional coach/support teacher on an individual basis
- Be observed by mentor to include a pre- and post-conference (mentor/mentee responsibility)
- Observe other classrooms with instructional coach/principal/support (if possible before starting and once in the classroom)

2nd Quarter of teaching = 4th Quarter of school year:

- Continue to meet weekly with mentor (mentor/mentee responsibility)
- Continue weekly reflection opportunity (coach/mentee)
- Work with the instructional coach/support teacher on an individual basis
- Be observed by mentor to include a pre- and post-conference (mentor/mentee responsibility)
- Self-video observation with reflection

Late Hire Checklist #13

(New hire did not go through orientation.)

Building Administrator
MIP (Most Important Points) about:
- Building expectations
    - Students leaving class
    - Supervision
    - Arrival/leave times
    - Classroom management/behavior issues
    - Curriculum expectations/instruction
    - Emergency situations
    - Contacting parents
    - Lesson plans
    - Most common ways communication is provided
    - Attire
    - Cell phones
- Eval process
- If need to call in sick/take personal day
- Access to shared drives/added to email lists/any building wide technology
- Confidentiality
- Professionalism
- Professional development expectations

School Building Office
- Room key
- Mailbox label
- Name outside door (new hire)
- Share their role & how they can assist

Department Chair
- Copies of textbook & teacher's edition
- Department shared resources
- Curriculum resources
- Overview of assessment plans-unit/semester
- Department processes
    - Grading policy
    - Ordering supplies
- Introduction to collaborating teachers

Counselor
- 504 plans
- Introduce-share role/any student concerns
- Confidentiality reminders
- Grade support information

SPED Teacher
- Introduce self to new person
- Discuss students with IEPs & accommodations
- Understand the roles of support staff

District Office
- District login information
- Health insurance
- Paycheck info
- Personnel policies (leave days)
- Access to policies-location
- Health insurance/employment paperwork
- Building keycard

Other Considerations
- Updated attendance roster
- Current seating chart in place
- Contact technology department for copy machine code access
- Where to park

(Other side info)

S.H.I.N.E. Brochure

S.H.I.N.E.
New Teacher Induction Program

Program Objectives

✓ To recruit and retain highly qualified educators in our district

✓ To integrate new teachers into the culture and climate of our schools, school district, and community

✓ To assist beginning teachers to manage the challenges that are common to all new teachers

✓ To enhance new teachers' professional development through reflection on their practice and student learning

Program Overview

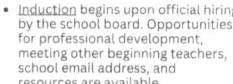

- **Induction** begins upon official hiring by the school board. Opportunities for professional development, meeting other beginning teachers, school email address, and resources are available.
- **Two days of orientation before school begins.** This includes classroom time with a mentor, technology training, elementary and secondary model classroom experience, and learning district expectations in a fun and engaging team-building time.
- **Six induction seminars** throughout the school year—two full-day workshops and three after-school sessions. (During the day, workshops are held at off-campus locations to expose teachers to community resources and assets.)
- A **bus tour** is conducted by the leadership team, which familiarizes new teachers with the culture and community of the district.
- **End-of-year recognition celebration** with mentors, administrators, and school board members. This is a formal program with video clips highlighting the year with many laughs and memories.
- A **mentor** in the same grade level or content area.
- **Classroom visits and support** with the full-time district S.H.I.N.E. coaches and weekly reflection opportunities.
- **Resource books** on classroom management and successful teaching components, including our book, The First Days of School.
- **Weekly collaboration** in the Professional Learning Community within grade level/subject area during late start Monday collaboration.
- **Classroom release opportunities** to observe other teachers and a monthly newsletter with instructional ideas.
- Access to **online professional development** resources.
- Organized **social events**.
- Show of **community business support** to familiarize teachers with community businesses.
- Updates and invitations to attend **local events or activities** in the community.

Moberly School District

Supporting Helping & Inspiring
New Educators (S.H.I.N.E.)

The Spartan Way-Excellence for All

www.moberlyspartans.org

S.H.I.N.E. was established in the fall of 2008 to provide a systematic support system for new teachers.

References

Berger, W. (n.d.). *How "Vuja de" Questioning Can Help You See the World Differently*. A More Beautiful Question. https://amorebeautifulquestion.com/power-of-vuja-de/

Cambridge English Dictionary: Definitions & Meanings. (n.d.). Cambridge Dictionary. https://dictionary.cambridge.org/us/dictionary/english/

Crowley, S. (2015, March 9). *Real-Life Tips and Stories for Mentors and New Teachers*. The Great Books Foundation. https://www.greatbooks.org/real-life-tips-and-stories-for-mentors-and-new-teachers/

Duggins, A. (2018, August 7). *4 Ways to Support Beginning Teachers*. NASSP. https://www.nassp.org/2018/08/07/4-ways-to-support-beginning-teachers/

Hirsch, A. S. (2017, August 10). *Don't Underestimate the Importance of Good Onboarding*. SHRM. https://www.shrm.org/topics-tools/news/talent-acquisition/dont-underestimate-importance-good-onboarding

Kachur, D. S., Stout, J. A., & Edwards, C. L. (2013). *Engaging Teachers in Classroom Walkthroughs*. ASCD.

Knight, J. (2018). *The Impact Cycle: What Instructional Coaches Should Do to Foster Powerful Improvements in Teaching*. SAGE Publications.

Knight, J. (2023, June 1). *The Close Watch: Developing the Art of Noticing Students*. Instructional Coaching Group. https://www.instructionalcoaching.com/blog/the-close-watch

Knight, J., & DeWitt, P. (2023, June 20). Coaching Conversations with Jim Knight [Host Jim Knight engages a conversation with Dr. Peter DeWitt]. In *Instructional Coaching Group* [podcast]. https://www.instructionalcoaching.com/resources/podcast

Moir, E. (1990). *Phases of First-Year Teaching* [Newsletter]. California Department of Education. https://resources.finalsite.net/images/v1609875581/k12albemarleorg/zwxzvuxk41tj8p7c2pqv/PhasesofFirstYearTeachersText.pdf

Scott, K. (n.d.). *Promoting Social-Emotional Learning for Our Teachers*. Learning Disabilities Association of America. https://ldaamerica.org/lda_today/promoting-social-emotional-learning-for-our-teachers/

Shaker, K. (n.d.). The power of vujà dé. *PM Network,, 29*(1), 25. https://www.pmi.org/learning/library/power-vuja-de-9430

Sinek, S. (2009). *Start with Why: How Great Leaders Inspire Action*. Portfolio. TED. https://www.ted.com/talks/simon_sinek_how_great_leaders_inspire_action?language=en

Spalding, A. (2024, May 1). *The Ultimate Guide to Reflective Practice in Teaching* [Blog]. https://blog.irisconnect.com/uk/blog/5-benefits-of-encouraging-teacher-self-reflection

Stroud, G. (2017, February 3). *Why Do Teachers Leave?* ABC. https://www.abc.net.au/news/2017-02-04/why-do-teachers-leave/8234054

Thomas, L., & Beauchamp, C. (2011). Understanding new teachers' professional identities through metaphor. *Teaching and Teacher Education, 27*(4), 762–769. https://doi.org/10.1016/j.tate.2010.12.007

Turner, D. A. (2019, October 19). *Former Chick-fil-A VP Dee Ann Turner: Want Your New Hires to Succeed and Thrive? Do This*. https://finance.yahoo.com/news/former-chick-fil-vp-dee-110027240.html

For Product Safety Concerns and Information please contact our EU
representative GPSR@taylorandfrancis.com
Taylor & Francis Verlag GmbH, Kaufingerstraße 24, 80331 München, Germany

www.ingramcontent.com/pod-product-compliance
Lightning Source LLC
Chambersburg PA
CBHW070402240426
43661CB00056B/2511